Praise for *What Every Christian Needs to Know About the Jewishness of Jesus*

"Jews and Christians need to talk with one another, but to do this each must listen to the other side. Many Christian scholars today have made colossal progress in grappling with Jewish sources and in listening to the variety of Jewish communities. Evan Moffic has stepped up the listening skills needed by the Jewish community to the voice of the Christian community. How has he done this? By going to the very source of the Christian faith—to Jesus himself, the Jewish teacher of Galilee in the first century. Moffic has accepted the challenge of seeking to explain Jesus as one who is best understood by understanding him as a Jewish teacher rooted in the Tanakh and the Jewish traditions. Christians will not all agree with everything Moffic says, but they will say he has listened well. For that alone I am immensely grateful for this book."
—Scot McKnight, theologian, speaker, and best-selling author of *The Jesus Creed*

"From the moment my parents dove head-first into their new Christian faith, I knew the name 'Jesus.' He was as much a part of my childhood as my little brother. The Jesus I grew up with was intelligent and wise, compassionate and kind. But it took adulthood for me to understand he was also Jewish. That revelation opened a world of insight I'd before missed. As I grew to know the real Jesus—a Jewish Jesus—my faith developed fresh depth and life. If you have a passion for learning, if you enjoy the stretch of good dialogue and aren't afraid of venturing into new territory, pull up a chair. I have two rabbis I want you to meet."
—Michele Cushatt, author of *Undone: A Story of Making Peace with an Unexpected Life*

"Thank you, Rabbi Moffic! As a Christian and a Catholic priest, I am grateful for the intriguing look into the Jewish life of Jesus. As such, this book is a wonderful gift to Christians who seek to further the rich faith and culture out of which Jesus emerged."

—Father Tom Hurley, pastor, Old St. Patrick's Church, Chicago

WHAT
EVERY CHRISTIAN
NEEDS TO KNOW
ABOUT
THE
JEWISHNESS
OF JESUS

~~~~~~~~~

A NEW WAY
OF SEEING THE
MOST INFLUENTIAL
RABBI IN HISTORY

~~~~~~~~~

RABBI EVAN MOFFIC

Abingdon Press
Nashville

WHAT EVERY CHRISTIAN NEEDS TO KNOW
ABOUT THE JEWISHNESS OF JESUS
A NEW WAY OF SEEING THE MOST
INFLUENTIAL RABBI IN HISTORY

Copyright © 2015 by Evan Moffic

All rights reserved.

Macro Editor: Lauren Winner

Library of Congress Cataloging-in-Publication Data

Moffic, Evan, 1978-
  What every Christian needs to know about the Jewishness of Jesus : a new way of seeing the most influential rabbi in history : / Rabbi Evan Moffic. — First [edition].
    pages cm
  ISBN 978-1-4267-9158-1 (binding: soft back) 1. Jesus Christ—Biography. 2. Judaism—History—Post-exilic period, 586 B.C.-210 A.D. 3. Jesus Christ—Jewishness. 4. Jesus Christ—Jewish interpretations. I. Title.
  BT301.3.M64 2016
  232.9'06—dc23

2015030744

16 17 18 19 20 21 22 23 24—10 9 8 7 6 5 4 3 2 1

MANUFACTURED IN THE UNITED STATES OF AMERICA

CONTENTS

Contents

FOREWORD

On the first day, of my first Rabbinic Judaism class, the first thing the rabbi said was, "The Torah has seventy faces." I could feel my heart getting bigger. As a Christian, I had never heard of the Bible being spoken of as a sacred text with many interpretive layers. I had never heard a religious person taking delight in asking questions and even challenged the stories and words of the Bible. My small religious starting place began to break open. It was in Jerusalem that I started to learn about the Bible and about Jesus from Jewish voices, well outside my tradition.

It is very good news, that the blond-haired, blue-eyed Jesus, who is wearing a bathrobe, is receding from view among many contemporary Christians. A more Jewish and authentic Jesus is being taken seriously. And discovering a Jewish Jesus is not just an academic exercise; it has widespread implications for the health of Christianity. In some sense, we cannot claim Jesus as our own anymore. He was Jewish, we need to hear him in his own Jewish context, and we need to hear from Jewish voices about how they read this rabbi from Galilee.

Personally, I learned more from my Jewish brothers and sisters about Jesus and his world than I ever learned in church.

And as a pastor, I see tremendous value in more and more Christians beginning a serious, authentic, gracious, and honest conversation about the person at the center of their faith with Jewish people at the table. Rabbi Evan Moffic's book brings a Jewish perspective on Jesus to the table in language that is powerful, straightforward, and conversational. Not everyone can move to Jerusalem or take an academic course on early Judaism, but everyone can read this book.

I also believe, from my experience with my Jewish friends, that a conversation about one's Jewish faith also benefits from a fresh look at Jesus. To see Jesus in his own context is to see him in conversation with the very beginning of Rabbinic Judaism. Jesus came from the same word as Hillel and Akiva.

I believe in the power of conversation. I believe we are better people of faith when we bring our experience into a real conversation with those from other faith perspectives and convictions. The Jewish-Christian dialogue is not a politically correct game. We are conversing about meaning and truth, beauty and love, family and forgiveness, and the mystery of God. What could be better!

I see this book as a brick in the bridge to a new future. As Christians and Jews begin to talk more honestly with one another about their faith something new is being born. On the one hand, a Jewish reading of Jesus, which takes many forms, is bound to rub against Christian convictions about Jesus. In other words, we are bound to disagree. On the other hand, Jewish perspectives on Jesus clarify, strengthen, and take further some Christian convictions about his mission, teaching, and life. In other words, we are bound to agree.

When we go deeper, as Christians and Jews, into the roots of our faith we see just how much we have in common, and we can see more clearly where our convictions differ. We cannot go further in Jewish-Christian dialogue without going as deep as we can in the tradition we are rooted in. We cannot learn new respect and compassion without seeing *both* what we have in common and where we part ways. If Christianity is going to grow up and not repeat the mistakes it made against the Jewish people, we have to make the effort to listen—really listen. And to listen to a Jewish perspective on Jesus is a lovely place to start.

This new era of Jewish-Christian dialogue is just dawning. In some sense, it's still very fragile. It started in academia and now is spilling out into the Synagogue and the Church. Rabbi Evan Moffic came to Mars Hill Bible Church one Sunday morning to have a real conversation with me about Judaism, in public, in front of three thousand people. This is seriously uncharted territory! I am grateful and inspired by his courage. This book takes another step toward furthering this important dialogue. We all must proceed with grace and an open mind. Plus, the kids in our pews are marrying one another, so we better learn to converse differently.

This book walks the reader through the essentials of Jesus' Jewishness. Even after years of studying Jesus' Jewishness, I found treasures and fresh insights in every chapter. I believe this book will inspire a deeper conversation with the reader's faith and curiosity and also raise new questions. Not many books have been written on Jesus by a practicing rabbi, with his own congregation, meant for Christians and Jews alike, who is deeply rooted in his own faith and also shows deep respect for Jesus and Christianity. In fact, this is the only one I know of. What a gift! Happy reading. And may you be inspired and encouraged to be a participant in the new era of Jewish-Christian dialogue.

Kent Dobson
Teaching Pastor
Mars Hill Bible Church
Author, *NIV First-Century Study Bible*

INTRODUCTION

A year ago I did a little experiment. I went to downtown Chicago, stood near a large church, and asked ten passersby a question. "Who started Christianity?" All ten of them answered "Jesus." I bet if I asked ninety more people, all ninety would give the same answer.

What they did not know—and what so many continue to miss—is that Jesus did not start Christianity. *Jesus lived and died as a Jew.* Christianity emerged after his death as an offshoot of Judaism, eventually separating and becoming its own religion. The beliefs and practices of this religion differ from Judaism, but they remain rooted in it.

What was first-century Judaism like? How did first-century Judaism help people approach God and draw holiness into their lives? When Jesus, a Jew, thought of God and Scripture and prayer, what kinds of things was he thinking about? By looking at the life of Jesus *as a Jewish life*, this book seeks to uncover the Jewish roots of Christianity. I want to hear Jesus the way his contemporaries—Jews in first-century Israel and Galilee—would have heard him. I want to understand him the way his Jewish contemporaries understood him. And I want to bring that understanding to twenty-first-century Christians and Jews.

These desires emerge from my own faith and vocation. I am a Jewish rabbi. As a rabbi I do not study Jesus in order to change my faith. Rather, I do so as someone who believes passionately in learning, growing, and sharing sacred truths with others. *I see myself as a guide for Christians and Jews through the landscape of first-century Judaism.* If, say, you are an American with Irish roots, and you were to visit Ireland, you would have an Irish guide take you through the towns and countryside. You would not expect an American guide. You would prefer a native Irishman.

The same is true for Christians who seek to deepen their faith by exploring their Jewish roots. The best guide is one who is a Jewish native. I live by the practices and traditions into which Jesus and his contemporaries were born. While this does not give me any special theological insight, it gives me a familiarity with the tradition and the texts and practices that grew into Christianity.

JOURNEY OF A LIFETIME

Why would anyone be interested in examining the Jewish roots of Christianity? Do those roots matter today? Absolutely. A few years ago my friend Reverend Lillian Daniel delivered a sermon titled "I'm Your Pastor and I Don't Care What You Believe." She suggested that contemporary Christianity has become too caught up on right beliefs rather than right action. Dogma has replaced duty, and the test of creed has become more important than the significance of deed. The solution to this overemphasis, she suggested, was a return to Christianity's Jewish roots. These Jewish roots gave early Christians an interpretative freedom and strong focus on good works.

Her sermon hit a nerve and quickly went viral. Its popularity suggests an openness and eagerness to deepen our faith by exploring its roots. This exploration is always enriching. Consider a person who goes to an opera. She can love the opera without knowing anything about the music or the story or the language of the songs. But if she knows a little bit about melody and harmony, if she reads the story beforehand, if she can look at a translation of the words, she will appreciate and understand the opera even more. The same is true with faith. When we learn, we grow.

As your guide, I have no agenda except your enrichment and enjoyment. The journey should be one of learning, growth, and depth. Too many of the books on the Jewish roots of Christianity have an agenda. They seek to "correct" people's misinterpretations of the Gospels. They seek to place ideas into the past that aren't there. They come from a place of confrontation rather than cooperation and friendship.

This book comes from a place of openness and learning. I have spoken in evangelical and mainline churches. I have studied with Christian ministers from across the theological spectrum. What unites all these encounters is a passionate interest in living a life of faith and knowledge. When Christians study and appreciate the Jewishness of Jesus, they begin to see Judaism not as a fossil or a museum. They see it as a living tradition that can challenge, teach, and change their lives. This book takes what I have learned from those experiences and puts it into the hands and hearts of all who seek to grow in faith.

A New Way to Meet Jesus

The heart of the book is the life of Jesus. We walk through his life from birth to death, looking at the way Jewish teachings, legends, and practices can illuminate each part of it. You will look at Jesus's birth from a new perspective, hear the Lord's Prayer with new ears, and find a renewed appreciation of Jesus's miracle-workings. You will understand what teachings Jesus had kicking around his brain when he discussed wealth, marriage, the Sabbath, and other laws at the heart of Judaism. In other words, when you encounter these Jewish teachings, you will meet Jesus differently. You will meet Jesus the Jew. My hope is that this meeting will resonate in your spiritual life, making you more aware of some of the ethical and political implications of Jesus's message and the ways that message has been interpreted and changed throughout history.

I wrote this book because I was frustrated and hopeful. I was frustrated by those who try to divide Jews and Christians into right and wrong, who try to keep alive an ancient conflict that has miraculously faded in our time. I was frustrated by those who write condescendingly about Judaism for Christians, trying to show the ways the Bible has always been "misread" and Christians "misinformed." I was frustrated by the disconnection between extraordinary scholarship on the Jewish background of Jesus and popular knowledge of it. I am hopeful that this book can serve as a bridge between the pulpit and the pew. I am hopeful that those who walk with Jesus can walk now with greater knowledge and love. I am hopeful that a contemporary rabbi can open up a new way of seeing the most influential rabbi in history.

CHAPTER 1

A HUMBLE BIRTH

A few years ago I read a story about a woman who had a painting in her home. She had purchased it at a garage sale for five dollars. (It had been marked eight, but the owner agreed to sell for five.) The painting hung in her home. She got used to it and didn't think much about it. One day a friend was over and began looking closely at the painting. The guest said to her friend, "Who's the artist?" The owner told her she did not know. The friend then said, "Well, it really looks like a Jackson Pollock." The owner was unfamiliar with Jackson Pollock, who is one of the twentieth century's most celebrated abstract artists. Soon, however, she visited a dealer and inquired about the painting. She discovered that it was, indeed, an original Jackson Pollock, and it was valued at $50 million!

Sometimes we do not know the value of what we have. This happens not only with art or physical goods. It can happen with a story or an idea. We can become so familiar and used to it that we forget how unique and extraordinary it really is. The birth of Jesus is among the most well-known stories in the world. Much of the world celebrates it every year on December 25. We celebrate it with elaborate pageants and displays. *Perhaps the familiarity of the story, however, has hidden some of its deeper meanings.* We may know it so well that we miss its depth. Indeed, when we look at it closely, we see that, from the setting to the language, every part of Jesus's birth narrative echoes parts of the Hebrew Bible (the Old Testament). Those echoes help us see the story in a new way. They illuminate profound lessons and implications threaded throughout the New Testament accounts of Jesus's birth.

Sometimes we have to do what is right rather than simply follow orders.

Let us begin with the setting. Jesus is born in an out-of-the-way guesthouse. He is then taken to a manger. It is a world away from the palace of King Herod in Jerusalem. Yet, Herod has heard of the coming birth. He does not know where it will take place, but he is aware something important is going to happen. Thus, he sends three "men from the East" to witness it. They arrive at the manger.

One of the cardinal rules of biblical interpretation is that the Bible does not include unnecessary details. Everything matters. Why, then, does the text reveal these details about Jesus's birth location? It could have just said Jesus was born and soon left for Egypt. What message is the emphasis on the birthplace meant to convey? It's meant to draw a parallel between the births of Jesus in Bethlehem and of Moses in Egypt. Indeed, the setting echoes the humble circumstances into which Moses was born. Moses was born while the Israelites were slaves in Egypt. Like Herod in Jerusalem, the Pharaoh in Egypt sus-

Abraham is standing at the entrance to his tent. It is a hot day, yet Abraham stands in the open flap of the tent. Suddenly he sees three men in the distance. They are approaching the tent. He rushes to greet them. He asks Sarah to prepare a meal for them. She does, and then Abraham serves it. They tell him that Sarah will soon deliver a child. Sarah overhears their remarks, and she laughs. The men then leave.

Yet, as they leave, we realize they were not really men. They were angels. Like the three wise men, they had been guided there by God, who sought to send Abraham and Sarah a message—his message of an impending miraculous birth. The birth is a miracle because Sarah and Abraham are in their nineties. A natural biological birth is impossible. The birth is ordained by God.

Why are the two stories so similar? Why are they told in this particular way? Determining the answer to this question can offer us an entirely new perspective on the birth of Jesus. The answer lies within several of the Jewish legends surrounding the angels' announcement to Abraham. It rests on the recognition that *Abraham was willing and eager to invite the angels into his tent. In other words, he was open to God's miracle.* He did not simply wait passively to receive it. He went out and invited it in.

Judaism—the faith of Abraham and of Jesus—is an active faith. We believe God lives where we let God in. Abraham let God into his tent. Joseph and Mary let God into the house. Had Joseph and Mary said, "This place is not fit for the birth of Jesus," or had they said, "Why should we let these three strangers into this place?" they would not have witnessed the miracle. Had Abraham not been standing in the opening of his tent—had he not rushed to provide hospitality to the three angels—he may never have been able to carry on the covenant through his son, Isaac. Miracles come to those who are ready to receive them.

The Jewish sages make this point in analyzing the way Abraham welcomes the three angels. They draw from his actions the religious imperative of hospitality. They point out that the story in Genesis begins with Abraham communing with God. Genesis 18:1 reads, "The Lord appeared to Abraham at the oaks of Mamre while he sat at the entrance of his tent." In other words, Abraham is experiencing a prophetic conversation with God while standing in the open flap of his tent. In the midst of this conversation, however, Abraham sees the three men approaching. He could have ignored them. He was in the midst of conversation with God! That's a pretty important activity. Yet, Abraham pauses his conversation so he can go out and welcome the visitors.

To put yourself in Abraham's shoes, imagine you are in a meeting with God in your home or office. Suddenly some visitors come by. Would you tell God to hold on so you can attend to the visitors? Does that not seem strange? Why would we put the needs of human visitors before the presence of God? Does that not strike you as disrespectful, even heretical? Not to the Jewish sages. They derived from Abraham's actions the following conclusion: "Greater is hospitality than receiving the divine presence."[1] They justified this conclusion because God approves of Abraham's behavior. After Abraham welcomes and feeds the guests, God resumes their conversation. And God uses the angels disguised as men to deliver God's message.

We need to remember that Abraham did not know they were angels. He simply saw three men approaching the tent.

His first priority was to attend to their needs. He exemplified the sacredness of hospitality. He met God where God wanted him to be. Abraham's willingness to challenge the conventional arrange-

Miracles depend on our faith, our readiness, our openness to receive them.

ment of power—to turn away from literally speaking to God to welcoming three strangers—is what made him great. As Rabbi Jonathan Sacks put it, "It is easy to receive the Divine Presence when God appears as God. What is difficult is to sense the Divine Presence when it comes disguised as three anonymous passersby. That was Abraham's greatness. He knew that serving God and offering hospitality to strangers were not two things but one."[2]

Almost exactly the same words could be said about Mary and Joseph. The function of the three wise men was not simply to meet the baby Jesus. It was to connect his divinity with his humanity. It was to demonstrate Mary and Joseph's openness to receiving the divine presence. Like Abraham and Sarah, who had upended their lives by responding to God's call to leave their homeland, Mary and Joseph had already shown their willingness to follow God's lead. Upon God's instruction, Joseph had married Mary. Mary had borne a "child from the Holy Spirit" (Matthew 1:18). Now they welcomed the three wise men whom God had sent. Their hospitality contrasts with the rejection they had received at the inn, where "there was no room" (Luke 2). Mary and Joseph witnessed a miraculous birth, as did Abraham and Sarah. They opened themselves up to the miracle through their hospitality. Miracles do not depend solely on God. They depend also on our faith, our readiness, our openness to receive them.

WELCOMING OUR OWN ANGELS

This truth applies not only to supernatural miracles like the ones we witness in the Bible. It works in our everyday lives. I saw this one day when I was visiting two sets of new parents in the hospital. Both were members of my congregation, and both had just given birth to their first child. The first set was relaxed and cool. They were focused on the baby's vital signs. They started to make phone calls to friends and family. The husband joked with me about starting the college savings fund. I had a pleasant visit and went down the hall. The next set of parents both had eyes filled with tears. They were tears of joy and awe. They spoke of the miracle they had experienced and asked me to say the *Shechyanu* prayer, which thanks God for having kept us alive to witness this moment.

These couples represent two perspectives that are not mutually exclusive but which do convey different approaches to life. One sees the events of birth as natural phenomena. The couple had intimate relations, and a child soon resulted from it. The other couple saw birth as a miracle, a gift from God that demanded gratitude and prayer. The difference between them is not *what* they experienced. It is the *way* they experienced it. One saw fact. The other felt faith. The Bible—whether we see it as literal fact or metaphorical truth—urges us to embrace the second perspective. How can we open ourselves up more to the miracles of life? How can we be more like Abraham and Sarah and Joseph and Mary? Who are the angels we need to welcome into our tents? What are the gifts we need to give and receive?

CIRCUMCISION AND FLIGHT TO EGYPT

Eight days after his birth, Jesus was circumcised. It is not clear who performed the circumcision, but since it was Jewish custom for a father to circumcise his son, it was likely Joseph. Male circumcision is a critical marker of Jewish identity. The practice began when Abraham circumcised Isaac on the eighth day of his life. Circumcision symbolizes the covenant—the sacred relationship—between God and the Jewish people. It represents the promises God made to Abraham, and Abraham to God. Understanding the significance of circumcision in Jewish tradition gives us greater depth of Jesus's teachings on salvation.

Circumcision almost always happens on the eighth day of a child's life. Abraham circumcises Isaac on the eighth day after his birth. The Torah gives no explanation for it, but it has become an ironclad custom in Jewish life. Even if the eighth day is Yom Kippur, the most sacred and solemn Jewish holiday of the year, the circumcision takes place. Even though the Torah does not explain the reason, later Jewish sages suggest the importance of the number eight. Eight is seven plus one. Seven represents the natural world, which is created in seven days, and one represents the one God who created the world. Seven plus one—eight—symbolizes the unity of the spiritual and physical worlds.

The deeper meaning of circumcision lies in the Hebrew word *brit*. The word *brit* is the term used for "ceremony of circumcision." It also means "covenant," that is, the promises between God and the Jewish people. In the Hebrew Bible, God promises Abraham two things: land and descendants. Jews throughout the centuries summarized the promise as survival.

No matter what happened, the Jewish people would survive. They would have a place to live and descendants to carry on the tradition.

At Mount Sinai, God makes a second covenant. This time it is with Moses and the people. They would not only have land and descendants but also follow a set of laws found in the Torah—the Five Books of Moses—and they would be God's "treasured possession," the chosen people. To be the "chosen people" is not to be a superior people. Rather, it is to have a relationship with God based on following God's law. It resembles a marriage. A husband or wife need not think his or her spouse is superior to every other person in the world in order to have a unique relationship with each other. Each is chosen by and for the other. In Judaism, the basis of this chosenness is observance of the Torah, given by God for the Jewish people.

The revelation of the Torah at Sinai makes the covenant between God and Israel a twofold covenant. The first part is with Abraham and refers generally to Jewish survival. It is rooted in biology and history. The Jewish people share a history. They are the children of Abraham and descend from the twelve sons of Jacob, also known as the twelve tribes of Israel. The second covenant—known as the Mosaic or Sinai covenant—is based on law. It is religious rather than historical, theological rather than biological. So Jesus's circumcision makes him part of that first covenant. His life is connected to the land of Israel and the Jewish people. He is a descendant of Abraham and the tribe of Judah. He also likely saw his life as part of the second covenant. He observed the Torah and followed Jewish law.

Jesus's circumcision also became a source for the apostle Paul's emphasis on the difference between law and spirit and between external and internal change. For Paul, the inward circumcision—what is called the "circumcision of the heart"—is far more important than circumcision of the flesh. This outward transformation is what makes one a true descendant of Abraham. As Paul puts it bluntly in Romans, "Since God is one, then the one who makes the circumcised righteous by faith will also make the one who isn't circumcised righteous through faith. Do we then cancel the Law through this faith? Absolutely not! Instead, we confirm the Law" (Romans 3:30-31).

This is a monumental verse because Paul redefines the meaning of being Jewish. While this verse has occasionally evoked criticism from Jews who see it as implying that Jews who are physically circumcised are only interested in external appearances, it does fit with a school of Jewish theology known as Prophetic Judaism.

PROPHETIC JUDAISM AND CIRCUMCISION

Prophetic Judaism is the voice in the Bible that critiques ritual and emphasizes justice and spirit. The Prophet Jeremiah, for example, frequently makes an argument similar to Paul's. "The time is coming, declares the LORD, when I will deal with everyone who is physically circumcised. . . . All these nations are really uncircumcised; even the people of Israel are uncircumcised in heart" (Jeremiah 9:25-26). In Prophetic Judaism, ritual and physical actions are not enough. They need to be driven by the spirit. Thus, Paul was drawing on a rich Jewish tradition when he emphasized circumcision of the heart rather than the body. His innovation was using this emphasis to remove physical circumcision as part of the definition of being Jewish. Prophetic Judaism never eliminated the requirement of physical circumcision. It simply said such a circumcision was not enough.

This distinction between the physical and the spiritual continues to challenge Jews and Christians. I once heard a pastor deliver a sermon critiquing Jews for believing the Old Testament text from Exodus demanded "an eye for an eye and . . . a tooth for a tooth." He went on to say that Jesus introduced a new element that spiritualized the meaning of this verse. Instead of requiring physical punishment for physical acts, Jesus taught that reward and punishment happen in the next life and that now we should love our enemies. The pastor contrasted the brute physicality of the Old Testament with the loving spirit of the New.

While Jesus and his followers did bring a focus on the loving spirit to matters of religious and civil law, they were drawing on a rich Jewish background in doing so. The Pharisees—a group often critiqued in the New Testament—interpreted the eye-for-an-eye text as referring to the idea of the punishment fitting the crime rather than mandating a literal eye for an eye or tooth for a tooth. They said a monetary fine could be an appropriate punishment for a physical crime. They also effectively outlawed the death penalty by requiring a nearly impossible amount of physical evidence in order to inflict it.

Knowing about Prophetic Judaism may unsettle some views. Many Christians have seen Jesus as overturning the world of law and strict justice as set out in the Old Testament. Here, however, we see the Gospel of Luke highlighting a central Jewish act of Jesus's life. It reminds us that Jesus was born a Jew, and to the next step of his Jewish journey we now turn.

CHAPTER 2

AN UNEXPECTED TURN

Philosopher Martin Buber once wrote, "All journeys have secret destinations of which the traveler is unaware."[1] Think about this truth in your life. Perhaps you dreamed of getting a certain job but ended up in a different one that you love. Perhaps you dreamed of living in a certain place but have found yourself in another city you can't imagine leaving. Perhaps you grew up in one faith tradition and now are part of another that feels absolutely right. We journey to places we may not glimpse until we arrive there.

We see this truth continually in the lives of the biblical heroes. They begin their journey with a destination in mind. Usually it is the Promised Land. But the real destination—the truths they are meant to embody and teach—seems to be something of which they are often unaware. In rare moments they may sense it, but it is in their unexpected journeys that the truth emerges. It is in the challenges they face that we learn the depth of their character and the purpose God had for them.

Consider the life of the patriarch Abraham. He begins his journey in Mesopotamia. He is told by God to make his way to the land of Canaan. He makes it there, but almost immediately, he is forced to leave. A famine sends him and Sarah scrambling to Egypt. Their son, Isaac, makes a similar journey from Canaan to Egypt. And then Isaac's son and grandsons also end up traveling to Egypt. All three patriarchs dreamed of living in the Promised Land, and all of them end up spending significant time in Egypt.

Jesus's journey follows a similar path. In the Gospel of Matthew, soon after he is born in Bethlehem, he is taken by Mary and Joseph to Egypt. They are fleeing King Herod, who is threatened by Jesus's birth. He fears that Jesus's future influence will bring instability to his kingdom. This journey is the first of many in Jesus's life. These journeys highlight the tension between home and exile, a theme appearing both in the Old and New Testaments. They also give us insight into the way God works. God works through people, and people, as Buber recognized, take circuitous routes to their destinations. For Jesus, the first stop on this route was Egypt.

DOES JESUS REALLY GO TO EGYPT?

The Gospels of Matthew and Luke give us different accounts. Luke says Jesus and family left soon after Jesus's birth and returned to their hometown of Nazareth. Matthew says Joseph and Mary took Jesus to Egypt after the three wise men had left. Numerous scholars have tried to make sense of these differing accounts. Some say both happened, and the text just does not give us all the details of the timing. For purposes of understanding Jesus's Jewishness, we do not need to know the exact details of what and how their journeys happened. We simply need to understand why the text tells us in the way it does that Jesus, Mary, and Joseph traveled to Egypt. In other words, knowing whether the journey to Egypt happened or not is less important than understanding why it is included in the Gospel of Matthew. To do that we need to tease out some connections between the story Matthew tells and the Old Testament.

The first connection is in the names of Jesus and his family: Jesus, Joseph, and Mary. These names are critical, and Matthew opens with a genealogy of Jesus including them. These three names help us understand the purpose of the genealogy. First, *Joseph*. He is a seminal figure in the Book of Genesis. Despised by his brothers, he is sold by them to traveling slave traders, who bring him to Egypt. He is the first from his family to spend a long period of time there. Joseph is particularly adept at having, remembering, and interpreting dreams. His insight into dreams helps predict the future, and it is through them that he predicts the Egyptian famine and saves the country. The Joseph of the New Testament is also a dreamer. A dream alerts him to the danger of their family staying in Bethlehem. Like his biblical namesake, this Joseph also has a father named Jacob! The name Joseph connects this story in Matthew linguistically and historically with the biblical Exodus story.

The name *Mary* is also important. Mary is derived from the Hebrew name *Miriam*. Miriam is Moses's sister in the Old Testament. She saves his life from the Egyptian Pharaoh by placing him in a basket and sending him down the Nile River. She also accompanies him into Pharaoh's palace by disguising herself as a nanny. Both the Old Testament's Miriam and

Matthew's Mary care for a child whose life is in danger by guarding and accompanying him in Egypt. A first-century Jew hearing the Gospel of Matthew would have immediately connected the names and the story with the Old Testament. He or she would have drawn a parallel between Jesus and Moses, and between Herod and Pharaoh, seeing Jesus as following in Moses's footsteps. He is not alone but is guarded and protected by those who love him, and he is destined for a critical role in redeeming Israel.

REDEMPTION AND SUFFERING

Why does the Bible want us to hear the story of the Exodus in the story of Jesus's flight to Egypt? Is there a lesson we are meant to see? There are several. First, we are to see that redemption requires suffering. Indeed, for both the Old Testament and the New, this redeeming of Israel could not happen without some experience of pain and anguish. The Israelites have to go down to Egypt and become slaves before God can redeem them. Jesus has to experience persecution and death on the cross before God can raise him up. The account of Jesus's journey to Egypt is the first example of the persecution he will face. The reason for their fleeing is Joseph's dream that Herod will find and kill Jesus. Matthew later reports that Herod had all the male children in Bethlehem age two years and younger slaughtered. The parallel with the Old Testament's account of Pharaoh murdering all the newborn Israelite males in

We teach the greatness of God by the way we live godly lives.

ancient Egypt is unmistakable. In the Old Testament, this massive slaughter of Israelite children plants the seed for God's intervening in Egypt. It is the catalyst for the Exodus.

The second lesson is more nuanced. Matthew wants us to draw a parallel between Jesus and Moses. He also wants us to see a profound connection between Jesus and the Old Testament's Joseph. We already saw a hint of connection in the names, but the parallel is much deeper. First, both Jesus and Joseph begin their life-saving work at age thirty. That is when Joseph becomes prime minister of Egypt and Jesus begins his public ministry. The church father Origen notes this in his commentary on Genesis. First-century listeners to the story of Jesus would also have recognized the age of thirty as one where the Israelite priesthood officially began, as noted in the Book of Numbers. It is the Old Testament Joseph's family that is associated with the Israelite priesthood.

A second parallel between Jesus and Joseph is the initial hostility of their peers. Joseph is despised by his brothers because their father clearly favors him, and he displays his arrogance. He tells them of his dreams of ruling over them and wears the special multicolored coat their father gave him. Their hostility leads his brothers into selling him to traveling Ishmaelite slave traders, which results in his arrival in Egypt.

We do not read about any initial hostility between Jesus and his siblings. Yet, he encounters hostility from his townspeople upon his return to the synagogue in Matthew 13, leading Jesus to say that a prophet is honored everywhere except his hometown. Like Joseph, Jesus is also beloved by his father, as we see emphasized through the Gospels. This love causes envy from others around him.

A third parallel is the connection between their gifts and the feeding of others. Joseph uses his ability to interpret dreams and predict the future in order to build up a reserve of grains and save Egypt from famine. When he reunites with his brothers, Joseph tells them that God intended him to come to Egypt to save many lives. Jesus also literally feeds the hungry at the wedding feast. This connection between prophecy, faith, and feeding is not simply physical. Joseph feeds future Jews by his extraordinary faith in God, and God's faith in him. For believers, Jesus also figuratively feeds the hungry. His death and resurrection become the bread of life because they give life to believers. First-century Jews would have seen in Jesus's life and heard in the Gospels echoes of the story of another of God's beloved, Joseph.

Of course, differences abound between the two. Joseph is never imagined as divine or as a purveyor of salvation. Jesus's role in the Gospels is much more significant than Joseph's in the Old Testament. Yet, believing in a divine savior similar to the biblical Joseph would not have been at odds with the worldview or expectations of first-century Jews. In fact, the Talmud records a belief in a precursor to the Messiah who was known as "the son of Joseph." This precursor will usher in the "Day of the Lord," which includes trials and tribulations and eventually leads to the arrival of the Messiah, the son of David. Later Christian theologians saw Jesus as combining these two functions. Tribulation (the crucifixion) is followed by salvation (the resurrection).

A final parallel is their resistance of temptation. The Gospel of Matthew tells the story of Jesus's temptations in the wilderness. Satan tempts him with worldly power, and Jesus rejects it. The Lectionary includes this reading for the first Day of Lent, a time often near the Jewish holiday of Passover, which celebrates the exodus of Jews from Egypt. It is in Egypt that Joseph also resists a worldly temptation. He is a servant in the household of a powerful Egyptian official named Potiphar. The name Potiphar means "dedicated to Ra," who is the sun god in Egypt. Thus, from an Israelite perspective, he is an idolater. Yet, Joseph works diligently for Potiphar and becomes his most trusted aide. Potiphar leaves his household under Joseph's management. Potiphar's wife, however, who is never given a name, attempts to seduce Joseph. He resists. She persists. Eventually, he has to flee the house to escape from her.

While the tempter in the stories of Jesus and Joseph are different, the symbolism is similar. Both Satan and Potiphar's wife use worldliness and idolatry as their temptation. Satan promises Jesus enormous earthly power. Potiphar's wife tempts Joseph with physical satisfaction—intimacy with a powerful Egyptian figure. Both resist these temptations as a sign of faithfulness to God. Interestingly, their fathers serve as important motivations in their resistance. As the son of God, Jesus is loyal to his Father. He challenges Satan's promise of earthly power by saying, "Go away, Satan, because it's written, 'You will worship the Lord your God and serve only him'" (Matthew 4:10). The Jewish sages say that when Joseph was tempted by Potiphar's wife, an image of his father, Jacob, appeared before him. That image reminded him of his loyalty to the God of Israel. Like Jesus, Joseph's resistance to temptation served, in the Talmud's phrase, to "sanctify the name of God."[2] In first-century Judaism, sanctifying God's name meant that one's behavior on earth reflected well on one's loyalty to God. In other words, we teach the greatness of our God by the way we behave on earth. As some of my Christian pastor friends have said, the greatest evangelistic tool is our own lives. We teach the greatness of God by the way we live godly lives.

WHAT THIS MEANS FOR US TODAY

As a rabbi I am amazed by the depth and ferment of Jewish life in the first century. The followers of Jesus were steeped in Jewish text and tradition, and they saw in Jesus parallels with several biblical figures. Much of Jewish life at the time was also in flux. While the Temple still stood and priests still oversaw sacrificial offerings, priestly power was diminishing. The Pharisees—a group of popular teachers often unfairly maligned in the Gospels for reasons we will discuss later—were gaining influence. In contrast to the priests, the Pharisees had a strong belief in the resurrection of the dead and arrival of the Messiah. While the apostle Paul says the Pharisees hunted down and persecuted followers of Jesus, it seems more likely that many of Jesus's early followers came from among the Pharisees, as Jesus's teachings would have resonated with their worldview.

I am also amazed by the contemporary relevance of the Old Testament's Joseph. In speaking at churches, I noticed people's ears would perk up when I started talking about Joseph. Now I see why. Not only do some of the actions and themes of his life parallel those of Jesus, but he also saved Jews and gentiles. Egyptians were not Jews, yet Joseph's planning for the famine saved all of Egypt. He is not the first Jew whose faith saved others. Abraham, for example, defended several other tribes, including that of the gentile priest Melchizedek. Yet, Joseph provided a model for Jesus in his role in saving Egyptians as well as Jews. He's an early sign of the universalism that would later distinguish Christianity from Judaism. Joseph was also betrayed by his brothers. He was one of twelve sons of Jacob, which is the model for the twelve apostles. They sell him into slavery. Yet, he emerges from that experience as a saver of lives. The same is true of Jesus.

For contemporary Jews and Christians, Joseph is also a wonderful model of reconciliation and co-existence. Joseph marries an Egyptian woman, creating the first interfaith marriage in the Bible. Yet, this marriage does not mean the end of his Jewish identity. Joseph's two sons become heads of their own Israelite tribes. Joseph also lives most of his life outside of the land of Israel. He participates and leads in non-Israelite society. Even today, most Jews live outside of the land of Israel. Joseph is a model for how to successfully integrate and live within two cultures. His significance for Christians only makes his relevance greater. One ancient interpretation with contemporary resonance is that of Caesarius of Arles. A French bishop in the sixth century, he interpreted Joseph's coat of many colors as a foreshadowing of the multitude of peoples that would later become followers of Jesus.[3] What is so profound about this interpretation is that the coat is originally a symbol of Jacob's favor for his son Joseph. But then it becomes a symbol of death when Joseph's brothers dip it in blood and show it to their father as proof for their lie that a wild animal devoured Joseph. Then for Caesarius it becomes a symbol of life in its foreshadowing of Jesus. Thus, a symbol of death becomes a prophecy of future life. While, as a rabbi, my own interpretation of the significance of Joseph's coat differs, I appreciate the beauty of this interpretation, as it adds another dimension to Joseph's religious significance. The more we study these texts together, the more our own faith and knowledge can deepen.

JESUS RETURNS

Whereas the Gospel of Luke does not tell the story of Jesus's journey to Egypt, it does give us the next glimpse into his childhood. Luke depicts the twelve-year-old Jesus teaching at the Temple in Jerusalem. The family had traveled there for the Passover holiday. Passover was one of the three pilgrimage holidays during which Jewish families would travel to Jerusalem to observe the festival at the Temple. Since the text tells us Jesus was age twelve, this visit may also have marked the time of his becoming a *Bar Mitzvah*. A Bar Mitzvah is a Jewish coming-of-age ceremony for young men that typically happens at age thirteen. The young man would typically say a blessing over the Torah (the first five books of the Old Testament, also known as the Five Books of Moses), read from it and also from one of the Prophetic books of the Old Testament, and teach about what he read. Although Jesus was not yet thirteen, it would not be unthinkable for a twelve-year-old to have a Bar Mitzvah ceremony. It happens in my own synagogue occasionally.

Becoming a Bar Mitzvah is part of the Jewish education Jesus would likely have received. That education starts at age three with study of Scripture and continues with study of the *Mishnah*—the first book of Jewish law—at age ten. The Bar Mitzvah at age thirteen marks a commitment to following Jewish law. Studies of the Talmud—commentary and discussion of Jewish law—begin at age fifteen. It typically takes place in a school known as a *yeshiva*, where students read and debate in pairs. Knowledge is displayed by memorization and interpretation of the text, including relating texts from different books to one another.

We do not know the extent of Jesus's Jewish education, but given how deeply Jewish teaching informs Jesus's adult teachings, it would probably have been extensive. Aside from the typical path of study beginning at age three, Jesus would likely have learned Hebrew. While Aramaic was the spoken language among Jews, students learned Hebrew for the purposes of prayer and study. He would also have become accustomed to the culture of debate in the yeshiva. He would also have memorized large parts of Scripture, which was the custom. The name of the first book of Jewish law—*Mishnah*—also means "repetition." Texts were learned through repetition and memorization.

Education also took place in the home. A father had a responsibility to teach his son Torah, and given his lineage, Joseph probably did so. Jesus clearly was a bright student. Luke depicts him debating with the sages and elders at the Temple. That is the context in which Joseph and Mary discover him after having lost track of him. According to Luke, Joseph and Mary lose track of Jesus soon after they arrive in Jerusalem. After failing to find him among the friends and relatives they were traveling with, they return to the Temple and find him "sitting among the teachers." While this story may seem fanciful—how could they lose Jesus and not realize it for two days?—it is not outside the realm of possibility.

While we do not know what texts and questions they were discussing, I think Luke's depiction serves two purposes. First, it establishes Joseph and Mary's interest and role in Jesus's Jewish education. They accompany him to the Temple, even thought they later lose track of him. Mary's presence is especially noteworthy, as mothers did not have the Jewish legal responsibility for a child's education, and she would not have been able to accompany Jesus into certain parts of the Temple. These parts of the Temple were inaccessible to women, though a special women's section also existed where men were not permitted. More importantly, it lends credence to the scholarly view that Jesus, Mary, and Joseph likely lived a lifestyle typical of Jewish families in Nazareth in the first century. That lifestyle would include observance of the Sabbath beginning at sundown on Friday evening, journeys to Jerusalem when possible for the pilgrimage holidays, tithing, holiday observance, thrice-daily prayer, and study. Prayer, as we will later see, focused on the Psalter.

The second purpose of this story is to establish Jesus as a rabbi. The title *rabbi* in first-century Judea and Galilee referred to a person who was knowledgeable in Jewish law. It did not require a certain sequence of education or knowledge of an extensive number of particular texts, as it does today. Rather, a rabbi was a respected Jewish scholar. A rabbi often served as a teacher and community leader as well, although these roles became more prominent in the second and third centuries of the Common Era (CE). Luke's depiction of Jesus studying and debating in the Temple suggests he received a thorough Jewish education. It is the only picture we have from Jesus's adolescent and young adult life.

IS IT OK TO CALL JESUS A RABBI?

Some writers and theologians have argued that Jesus was not a rabbi and do not emphasize the importance of his traditional Jewish education. Reza Aslan, for example, argues that Jesus was primarily a political zealot dedicated to overthrowing Rome. John Dominic Crossan argues that Jesus lived like a typical Mediterranean peasant frustrated with Roman rule and attracted to some of the smaller Jewish apocalyptic sects. Some scholars say it is inaccurate to refer to Jesus as a rabbi because the "rabbinic period" in Judaism began with the destruction of the Jerusalem Temple in 70 CE, long after Jesus's death. After 70 CE, the great teachers of the time were called "Rabbi." Before then, however, they were not.

I think calling Jesus rabbi is fine as long as we recognize that the title describes a cultural status rather than an official position. That is the way in which the Gospels use the title. They refer to Jesus as a "rabbi" or "my rabbi" several times. These references do not come exclusively from his disciples. They come from a lawyer, a large crowd, and a priest. In first-century Jewish culture, the title *rabbi* referred also to one's status as a guide and master. Disciples were guided by their masters, who were known as rabbis. A few decades after Jesus's death, as the discipleship process became more formalized, *rabbi* became a professional title. It underwent a similar process as the word *reverend*. Centuries ago, clergy were addressed as the "most reverend so and so." In formal settings, some still are. Over time, however, *reverend* became a title of its own and became a synonym for *minister*. During Jesus's time, however, *rabbi* was not an official title. It described the person's status and function. During the post–70 CE rabbinic period, however, it become an official title, but the function remained the same. Thus, we can say Jesus did serve as a rabbi, even though it had not yet become an official title during his life.

Jesus lived and grew up in a culture thick with textual study and piety.

Aside from his teachings and cultivation of disciples, which we will explore in subsequent chapters, knowing Jesus was a rabbi helps us understand the choreography of his life. His frequent travels from town to town were not an uncommon part of a rabbi's life. Rabbis would visit different synagogues and communities and stay in people's homes. Rabbis also had another occupation for which they were paid, since Jewish law did not permit people to earn a living from teaching. Some rabbis were blacksmiths. Others were shoemakers or coin minters. Jesus, as we know, was a carpenter. Rabbis also served as moral exemplars, showing humility and consistency in their behavior. One famed teacher lost his position as head of a major school because of his arrogance. Their responsibility was not just to teach and preach the Torah; they were expected to live it. This expectation helps explain why the Talmud—the primary rabbinic text—so frequently alludes to the Bible. Rabbis were expected to live the texts. As twenty-first-century rabbi David Wolpe put it, "Rabbinic documents are so densely allusive not because the rabbis were straining to display erudition, but because the rabbis were educated Jews and as such lived those texts. The stories and the laws of the Bible were common coinage. They were the yardsticks against which life was ceaselessly measured."[4] Thus, Jesus lived and grew up in a culture thick with textual study and piety. *In contrast to the surrounding Roman culture, whose ideal type was a warrior, he lived within a Jewish matrix whose ideal type was the scholar.* That is why we meet the young-adult Jesus, for the first and only time, as he is studying and debating with sages in the Temple.

WHY THIS STORY MATTERS TODAY

Part of the power of the story of the twelve-year-old Jesus in the Temple is that it makes him very human. He is a lost child. He loses track of time and gets caught up in doing what he loves doing—studying and debating the finer points of Torah. Many Jews today can relate personally to the experience of studying Torah at age twelve.

For Christians, the story of Jesus's tarrying in the Temple serves as a reminder of Jesus's Jewishness, and it also helps explain his frequent recourse to teaching. Jesus was imbued with the rabbinic culture of his day, which emphasized learning and knowledge. His parables and stories, as we will later see, emerge out of the experience depicted in Luke.

Once when I taught this text to a church group, several people asked me why Jesus would be studying and debating with elders. Did he not have peers? One way to answer would be to say that Jesus was a prodigy, and his knowledge and erudition justified his association with the elders. Another way to answer would be to point out that Moses also learned and drew from the wisdom of the elders. God instructs him to meet with the elders when he arrives in Egypt and before he meets with Pharaoh so he can gain their guidance and support.

My own answer, however, is more personal. When I was younger and attended synagogue, my parents sang in the choir.

Thus, I usually sat without them during worship. Eventually I came to sit with a group of elderly men who were longtime members and regulars at the synagogue. They knew the prayers and the Bible readings by heart. In fact, they knew the prayers so well they could say them with their eyes closed. They would whisper to me during the rabbi's sermons, frequently pointing out where they thought he was wrong! We would ask each other questions. Often we would continue our conversation during the fellowship hour after services. They became my mentors and teachers in Jewish community. A house of worship brings together people of different generations. One rabbi once said to me that Judaism is caught more than it is taught. In other words, we imbue what others around us are doing. We learn from people more than we learn from books. That's what was happening to me in the synagogue. And that's what might have been happening to Jesus in the Temple. He was learning not only from the prayers and Torah scroll. He was learning through the elders.

That learning must have been effective because the next major experience we see Jesus facing is the temptation in the wilderness. Like Abraham and like Moses, he is put to a great test. Had he learned and grown enough in his faith to pass it?

CHAPTER 3

ENTERING THE WATERS

Before we face a great challenge—start a new job, visit a dying parent, tell our partner something he or she doesn't want to hear, sit down at a big job interview—we need to get into the right frame of mind. We need to focus our minds and hearts. A beautiful Hebrew prayer preceding the reading of the Torah asks God "to purify our hearts so that we may serve you in truth." A more contemporary and perhaps prosaic example is in the Rocky Balboa movies. If you watch carefully, you see that Rocky always says a prayer in his corner of the ring before beginning the fight. He needs to get in the right frame of mind. Some football teams follow the same practice. The point, I believe, is not to convince God of anything. If asked, I think most of the players would admit that God does not have a preferred team. Rather, prayer brings out the best in us. It lifts up our spirits.

In a much broader way, the next two parts of Jesus's life follow this pattern. Jesus is about to face a major test of faith in the wilderness. To prepare for it, he undergoes an immersion in the Jordan River from a mystical prophetic figure named John the Baptist. This is known as his baptism. Then he spends forty days in the wilderness. These two incidents are both steeped in Jewish tradition. They reflect ancient texts and stories. They fit into the context of first-century Jewish life. They illustrate central themes like the coming of the Messiah and purification of the soul. Indeed, they continue to echo in Jewish and Christian practice today.

WHAT IS BAPTISM?

Baptism—the dipping of a person into a body of water as a means of some kind of spiritual purification—is rooted in the ancient Jewish practice of ritual immersion. To become ritually pure a person would immerse himself or herself in a pool of water known as a *mikveh*. The Hebrew word *mikveh* means "collection," but it has come to refer to a collection of water. Jewish law mandates that some of the water come from a natural source, such as a spring or groundwater or rain.

For several centuries before the time of Jesus, immersing oneself in a mikveh was a way to gain ritual purity. Ritual purity is not the same as physical hygiene, although they can be related. Neither does ritual purity convey any moral judgment or cleanse a person from sins. Rather, ritual purity is a state of being. It is constantly in flux. Menstruation, for example, makes a female impure for a period of time, as does nocturnal emissions for a man. Other sources of ritual impurity include contact with a dead body, sexual relations, skin disease, and unusual body fluids. The waters of the mikveh served to purify a person from these sources of impurity.

In order to serve this critical function in Jewish life, mikvehs were constructed throughout the land of Israel and other Jewish communities. Even today they are among the first items built in a new Jewish community. Even though it only served a Jewish legal purpose, ritual immersion did begin to develop a spirituality of its own, especially for women. It marked major life transitions. It served as a way of mourning and celebrating. Immersion in a mikveh might also serve as a ritual accompaniment for other religious acts like the offering of sacrifices or repenting of one's sins. It was such an important part of Jewish life that the sages included it alongside circumcision and sacrificial offerings as part of the requirements for a person converting to Judaism.

Part of its power came from the symbolism of water. For Jews, water represents life and Torah. In ancient Israel water was also a precious commodity, and the level of the Sea of Galilee often served as a bellwether for the national mood. Prayers for rain abound in the Talmud. The connection between water and Torah is also an ancient one. Like water, the Torah nourishes life. It satisfies the thirst for righteousness and closeness with God. Both water and Torah also come from God. They are among God's greatest gifts: the source for everything in life. Both the mikveh and the Torah have been called *mayim chayim*, a Hebrew phrase meaning "living waters." They are essential to physical and spiritual well-being.

Baptism emerges out of the practice of mikveh immersion. The word *baptize* simply means to dip in water. By the first century CE, baptism had become an essential part of the religious life of several Jewish sects, especially the Essenes. The Essenes were former Israelite priests who left the Temple for the more isolated environs of the caves of Qumran by the Dead Sea. They felt that the culture and practices of the Temple had become too corrupt, and they saw isolating themselves as the only way to survive. They awaited a messianic figure called the "Teacher of Righteousness." They mingled their concerns for ritual and moral purity in the practice of immersion. According to the historian Josephus, the Essenes would bathe in cold water in both the morning and evening as a means of attaining ritual purity and striving for holiness and total dedication to God.[1]

John the Baptist drew from and expanded this Jewish practice. He was familiar with the work of the Essenes. He also came from a priestly family and likely knew the laws of purity and impurity. The Essenes were an insular group, and scholars believe he may have broken off from the group to expand the practice and meaning of ritual immersion. How significant and influential a figure John was is an issue that divides scholars. What is clear, though, is that the Gospels see him as fulfilling an important role in the unfolding of Jesus's mission. For the Gospel writers he is the precursor to the Messiah. In particular, he is the successor—or some say the reincarnation—of the Old Testament prophet Elijah.

ELIJAH THE PROPHET AND JOHN THE BAPTIST

Elijah is a seminal figure in the Old Testament. He constantly preaches against idolatry. He prods the people toward repentance. That is the purpose of a story in 1 Kings. Elijah is challenged by the priests of a Canaanite God named Baal. He defeats them, and the Israelites immediately repent. "And when all the people saw it," we read, "they fell on their faces and they said: The LORD, He is the God; the LORD, He is the God" (1 Kings 18:39; my translation from the Hebrew). These exact words are repeated by Jews during the Jewish Day of Atonement, where we repent for sins committed during the previous year.

Tellingly, this biblical battle against and example of idolatry took place in the wilderness. Like John the Baptist, Elijah spends considerable time in the wilderness near the Jordan River, fed by ravens that bring him meat and bread. The wilderness holds a privileged place in Jewish tradition because it allows people to have an unfiltered experience of God. The wilderness lacks the distractions of the city, and in it people can hear clearly God's voice. Jewish wisdom also describes the wilderness as unclaimed territory. It is not ruled by a particular group or nation. Anyone can go there, just as anyone can learn from and embrace God's law. As one Jewish wisdom text puts it, "the Torah was given in public; given openly in a free place. For had the Torah been given in the land of Israel, the Israelites could have said to the nations of the world: You have no share in it. But now that it was given in the wilderness publicly and openly in a place that is free to all, everyone who wishes to accept it can come and accept it."[2]

The wilderness setting and focus on idolatry recur in the life and character of John the Baptist. His baptisms take place in the wilderness in the Jordan River. He challenges the Israelites of his day, even calling them a "brood of vipers" who are not worthy of their ancestor Abraham. John even dresses as Elijah did. The Gospel of Mark opens with a description of John baptizing Jews in the Jordan River. He is wearing "clothes made of camel's hair, with a leather belt around his waist" (Mark 1:6). In 2 Kings 1:8, we read a similar description of Elijah: "He wore clothes made of hair with a leather belt around his waist." Some Christian scholars see John as not just fulfilling the role of Elijah. He is actually Elijah himself, identified by a different name. The Gospel of Mark makes this very point in chapter 9.

Unlike some of Jesus's other experiences—the forty-day fast in the desert, for example— his baptism feels especially accessible to us.

These similarities tell us that some first-century Jews saw Jesus as fulfilling the role of the Messiah. Elijah— in the form of John the Baptist—has arrived, meaning that the Messiah is not far behind. John's suffering—he was beheaded by Herod—fits the biblical prophecies of suffering coming before the oncoming of the Messiah. John also performed the functions expected of the precursor to the Messiah. He chastised the people for their idolatry. He attained devout followers and enemies among the Jewish people. The Gospel of Luke highlights his connection with key Old Testament figures by describing his miraculous birth by the elderly Elizabeth and Zechariah. This birth echoes that of Isaac by the aged Sarah and Abraham. Jewish hearers of the Gospel in the first century would also have heard traces of Hannah's miraculous birth. In 1 Kings, Hannah goes to the Jerusalem Temple and pleads for a son. The priest Eli initially thinks she is drunk, but when he hears her lament, he says God will cause her to conceive, which she eventually does. She dedicates that son, Samuel, to divine service and then sings a song of joy that Mary will echo later in the Magnificat in Luke 1. Samuel plays a critical role in biblical history as the one who anoints King David. Similarly, John the Baptist will be the one who announces the arrival of David's descendent Jesus.

From a literary point of view, John the Baptist also connects the Old and New Testaments. Since Mark is the earliest of the Gospels, and John appears right at the beginning of Mark, he is the closest New Testament figure to the Old. His connection with Elijah also echoes the Old Testament. Indeed, some Christians see John the Baptist as the last of the Hebrew prophets under the "Old Covenant." Jesus introduces the New Covenant and becomes its central prophet. John is the link between the Old and the New. He is part of the Old Covenant, as he precedes Jesus. Yet, in announcing Jesus's role, he connects the Old and the New.

JESUS'S IMMERSION

In addition to announcing Jesus's arrival and connecting it to the Old Testament, John baptizes Jesus, dipping him into the Jordan River. This immersion comes at Jesus's request, as John wonders whether he is worthy to immerse the Son of God. Jesus insists, however, and his immersion is followed by the appearance of a dove and a heavenly voice saying, "This is my Son whom I dearly love; I find happiness in him" (Matthew 3:17). This text bristles with Jewish reference and significance. The first is God's describing Jesus as "my Son." This description echoes the creation of semidivine beings in Genesis 6:1-4, where angels seem to impregnate human females. We see this ancient Near Eastern idea in Greek mythology as well. More importantly, however, it echoes the Book of Exodus's depiction of the entire people Israel as God's beloved son. When God speaks to Pharaoh through Moses, God orders him to "let my son go," referring to the Jewish people (Exodus 4:23; my translation from the Hebrew). When Pharaoh ultimately does not, God inflicts death upon the firstborn sons of Egypt. This reciprocal divine punishment indicates one of the ways the biblical authors saw the relationship between God and Israel. Israel is the firstborn son of God. The purpose of the Exodus is to bring redemption to God's beloved son Israel. The Gospels add a new chapter to this story by using God's son, Jesus, to bring redemption to the world.

While the Old Testament generally saw the people of Israel as referring to the son of God, it does occasionally refer to sole individuals in that capacity. In 2 Samuel 7, God promises that an heir of King David will remain on the throne forever and will be a "son to me" (v. 14). As understood here, the king is not a physical son of God. Rather, he is adopted or rebirthed as God's son. In introducing Jesus as the son of God, Mark is drawing from this view. First-century Jews would probably not subscribe to the idea of immaculate conception, which is a theological theme introduced later. In other words, the description of Jesus as God's beloved son would have made sense as a biblical echo, not necessarily a biological statement.

First-century Jews would also not be surprised by the story's describing the voice of God speaking over Jesus's baptism. It echoes the creation story, where God hovers over the waters and speaks the world into being. The world is born through God's voice. So, in the Gospels, is birth of a new world signaled through God's voice over the water in which Jesus is immersed. The divine voice also indicates God's active participation in the affairs of humanity. In the Talmud the *bat kol*—divine voice—is heard at critical moments. When a group of rabbis debates the nature of their authority, for example, a divine voice intervenes to establish that majority rules when deciding a ritual question. The *bat kol* draws attention to a critical development, and its presence would have alerted Jews that this was no ordinary baptism. It establishes in public the significance of Jesus's purpose.

I know some people find this emphasis on divine voice strange. Does God really speak aloud? When people claim today to hear God's voice speaking aloud, we are more likely to question their sanity than follow their teachings. Yet, the Gospels reflect a common Jewish belief of the time. God did speak at critical moments. Those moments were much rarer than in the biblical past. In the Hebrew Bible God speaks frequently to both Jews and gentiles, including the pagan prophet Bilaam. Over the course of the Hebrew Bible, however, God's voice appears less often. By the time we get to the Book of Esther—by most scholarly accounts the final book of the Bible composed—the word *God* is absent from the text. The Pharisees—who preceded the rabbis—believed God's voice was most often heard through study of the Bible rather than a direct auditory experience. As one contemporary rabbi said, "When I pray, I speak to God. When I study, God speaks to me."[3] Still, in first-century Israel, at critical moments, the voice could be heard. Mark describes Jesus's baptism as one of those moments.

WHY AT THE MIKVEH?

Why did God decide to speak at that particular moment? God could have chosen any moment to speak directly to Jesus. Why at baptism? I think the reason God chose to speak at Jesus's baptism rests in what the Jewish tradition teaches about water. Water symbolizes life—and it also symbolizes Torah. The two go together. Just as water feeds our bodies, Torah nourishes our spirits. Key moments in Jewish history happen around water, most notably the splitting of the Red Sea. Israelites pass through the water—immersing themselves without getting wet—as their means of liberation and redemption from Egypt. In baptizing people out in the wilderness, John the Baptist was effectively reenacting the Exodus from Egypt and entry into the Sinai wilderness. During Jesus's time, baptism was not seen exclusively as a means for repentance for sin. It was spiritual transformation, a redemptive reliving of the Exodus story.

God also chose to speak to Jesus at the immersion in part because baptism was an experience that most human beings can relate to. Even someone who has never been baptized or immersed in a mikveh knows the cleansing role of water, and we know spiritual transformations can happen when we immerse ourselves in a ritual. So unlike some of Jesus's experiences—the forty-day fast in the desert, for example—that are harder for ordinary people to relate to, Jesus's baptism feels especially accessible to us. God may have spoken to Jesus then in order to convey to us, centuries later, "You too might hear from me, perhaps in the midst of a ritual or perhaps when you encounter revivifying, cleansing water."

The Jewish sages point out that immersion in the mikveh also reenacts physical birth. The pool of water recalls the state we knew before we were born. The ritual of entering and leaving the waters creates the time and space to transform ourselves. Another Jewish teaching reinforces the role water plays in our development. The Talmud teaches that parents needs to teach their child at least three things: Torah, a trade, and how to swim. Swimming may seem prosaic in light of the obvious significance of the other two. Yet, swimming demands we enter the water, control ourselves, and emerge whole from it. Swimming symbolizes both dependence and independence. The water, like God, holds us up. Yet we need to know how to keep ourselves afloat. When we enter the living waters of the mikveh or the baptismal fount, we reenact both our birth and our journey to develop into who we are meant to be.

Understanding the meaning of baptism in ancient Judaism helps us see why we encounter the story of Jesus and John the Baptist so early in the Gospels. For early followers of Jesus, the baptism marked the start of his formal ministry. It is only after the baptism that he encounters God in the wilderness, as we will see shortly. It is only after the baptism that he finds disciples. It is only after the baptism that followers recognize him as and call him Messiah. Jesus is becoming who he is meant to be.

John the Baptist not only serves as the precursor to the Messiah—the incarnation of Elijah the Prophet but also

Jews might call the life-giving power of water the Shekinah, or *the living presence of God. Christians might call it the Holy Spirit.*

helps us understand the different expectations first-century Jews had for the role of the Messiah. John and Jesus represented different groups within first-century Judaism. Both groups yearned for a Messiah. The strength of the Roman Empire and its increasing presence and persecution of the Jewish people sparked this hope among many. As James Carroll points out in his book *Christ Actually*, times of conflict heighten messianic expectations. Just as the Maccabean war in the second century

BCE led to yearnings for a Messiah who would destroy the Seleucid empire, so the increasing tension with the Romans primed yearnings for a Messiah among first-century Jews.

John the Baptist came out of the apocalyptic tradition that began during the Maccabean period. It was during that time that a group of priests—who would come to be known as the previously discussed Essenes—left Jerusalem and set up a pious community near the Dead Sea. Their language—as illustrated in the Dead Sea scrolls—was revolutionary and extreme. They saw the world in starkly black-and-white terms. Judgment day was coming soon, and the Messiah would be the one indicating its imminent arrival. "The Day of the Lord"—a phrase appearing frequently in the Bible—was for them a cataclysmic event. It would usher in an end to Israel's suffering and bring about the reign of the one God on earth.

Some Jews during the first century likely saw John the Baptist as fulfilling this messianic role. He may have been seen as the "Teacher of Righteousness" whom the Dead Sea scrolls describe. He appealed to those expecting an apocalyptic event. His extreme language and appearance heightened his other-worldliness. He symbolized the imminent arrival of God's reign on earth. The end of days would happen any day now.

This apocalyptic thinking did not play as prominent a role in the ministry of Jesus. The kind of Messiah Jesus's followers expected would not introduce a radical break with the present. The Messiah would not appear as a zealot or religious extremist. Rather, as the Gospel of Luke points out, "Nor will people say, 'Look, here it is!' or 'There it is!' Don't you see? God's kingdom is already among you" (Luke 17:21). Yes, one can find other texts in the Gospels expecting a more apocalyptic role for Jesus. Yet the general thrust, consistent with

Jewish tradition, was that the kingdom of God would not mark a radical break with the present. Several scholars suggest the rupture between Jesus and John the Baptist was due to this fundamental difference in perspective. As James Carroll puts it,

> The apocalyptic dualism that readily divided the good from the evil, typified by the preaching of John the Baptist, is nowhere in evidence in the Jesus of the Gospels, who associates with sinners and affirms the delights of ordinary life. Indeed, the break between Jesus and John the Baptist, which all four Gospels report, may be the great clue to what kind of apocalyptic figure Jesus was and what kind of Kingdom he preached.[4]

Both John and Jesus expected a transformation of the world. Yet, Jesus saw it coming slowly and broadly. John saw it arriving sharply and only through the efforts of the truly pious. Both views had many supporters in first-century Judea and Galilee.

A LIVING FAITH

Even as John the Baptist preached and envisioned escape from the world, however, the ritual he performed enhanced life within it. Remember, the waters of both a baptism and a mikveh are known as *mayim chayim,* or living waters. This phrase echoes both physical and spiritual truths. The physical truth is that water is life. Without water, we will not live. Out of water, we begin life. Our bodies are made up of water and are sustained by water.

The spiritual truth lies in the symbolism of the water. It nourishes life. We can be moved by the beauty or sound of the ocean. We can be awed by the power of a waterfall. Even more viscerally, however, we can feel the life-giving power of the water. Jews might call this power the *Shekinah*, or the living presence of God. Christians might call it the Holy Spirit. Water can rearrange the way we see the world.

About three years ago I witnessed this power in a visceral way. I accompanied a new mother and her baby to the mikveh. Both the mother and the baby were converting to Judaism. The child's father (the woman's husband) was Jewish, but the mother was not (and so, in keeping with the Jewish teaching that Jewishness passes through the mother, neither, technically, was the baby). I had performed their wedding a few years earlier. We had prepared for the experience of the joint mother-child immersion in the mikveh and conversion to Judaism. We had studied Jewish history and holidays. They had come to worship at the synagogue. They had shared the Sabbath and holiday meals. We had talked about everything that would happen at the mikveh. In privacy she and the baby would undress and, accompanied by the female director of the mikveh, she would undergo three immersions in the small pool of water. After each immersion she would say a blessing. Her husband and I were behind a wooden screen and could hear the splash of the water as she dunked down and the blessings. After all of these steps, her conversion would be complete.

The ritual began normally. Mom and baby immersed in the water, came up, and said the first blessings. They did so twice more. Then, after the third immersion, the mom asked if she could say a personal prayer. We said yes. She began to weep and speak of her parents, grandparents, and ancestors—of all those who had raised her with a love of God that made this decision possible. She spoke of the beauty she found in her husband's (and now her) Jewish traditions. She spoke of her dreams for her child.

Both her husband and I knew God was speaking through her at that moment. Normally a reserved woman, the combination of waters, the blessings, and her family opened her heart and soul. An ancient tradition marked the beginning of a new phase of life. It brought to life a dormant faith inside her. The waters bring life to the spirit. They are also meant for this life. Baptism is often understood by Christians as a way of attaining eternal life. I see this in interfaith couples I counsel who are ambivalent about getting their child baptized. Quite often a parent is pressing them to do so even if they are unsure about the religious tradition in which they are going to raise the child. The concerned parent simply wants to make sure the baby is assured of some kind of eternal life or salvation.

Yet, in its original Jewish understanding, baptism was about life in this world. It was about beginning a new phase of life—be it after repenting for one's sins, after taking on a new set of beliefs, or after getting married or becoming a parent. It was about making life sacred. Most people did not just visit John the Baptist or another baptizer and leave. They made regular return visits. For Jews, the mikveh is still used in this way. Perhaps this perspective can enhance Christian practice as well. The spirituality of the experience can be both momentarily overwhelming and eternally transformative. It can combine the physical and spiritual. As one recent writer put it, describing her feeling as she emerged from immersion in the mikveh, I "was placed in the hands of the three mothers, who . . . energetically massaged and kneaded my flesh with skilled hands, stimulating all my five senses to the edges of their nerve endings. . . . I was flooded with an elemental emotion so stunning in its intensity, so acute, it was as if every fiber of my being was stirring wondrously to life."[5]

As it did for so many others, immersion in living waters began a new phase in Jesus's life. He left the waters and began the next part of his journey. This journey resembled that of the ancient Israelites. They left the Red Sea and entered into the Sinai wilderness. Similarly, Jesus leaves the Jordan River and enters into the wilderness. This part of the journey brought new challenges and temptations. To them we now turn.

CHAPTER 4

SURVIVING A WILDERNESS OF TEMPTATIONS

The Jewish New Year is known as *Rosh Hashanah*, which means "Head of the Year." It is celebrated in the synagogue with a worship service and a reading from the Torah. The Torah reading tells the story of God asking Abraham to take his son, Isaac, up to the top of Mount Moriah. There he is to slaughter Isaac as an offering to God. Abraham obliges. He takes his son and begins the journey up the mountain. When they get to the top, he binds Isaac to an altar. He raises the knife and then, at the last moment, an angels stays Abraham's hand. The angel tells him God does not want the murder of his beloved son. God, the angel tells Abraham, was testing him. God wanted to see whether Abraham would truly obey the divine word. Abraham did, the angel says, and therefore God will reward him with devotion and prosperity.

This story probably bothers you, as it does me. Every year on Rosh Hashanah at least half a dozen members of my congregation ask me why we still read this story. Isn't it archaic? Isn't it barbaric? Why does God need to test Abraham? And why is the test so horrific?

I occasionally tell them there are no good answers to this question. Some rabbis suggest Abraham failed the test! They say God wanted Abraham to say, "No! I will not sacrifice my son. I will not perform an immoral command, even if it comes from God." This minority view, however, is generally subordinate to the argument of Søren Kierkegaard, who said Abraham exemplified the meaning of faith by following this outrageous command. He suspended his ethical judgment and followed God's will. Kierkegaard therefore called Abraham the "Knight of Faith."

I believe neither of these views adequately deals with the story of the binding of Isaac. We do not know what God was trying to teach Abraham. We do not know whether Abraham passed or failed the test, though the text does suggest he passed it. What we do know is that *we are all tested in life*. We are tested by our peers. We are tested by our families. We are tested in our responsibilities. We are tested by temptation.

After leaving the community of John the Baptist, Jesus faces several spiritual tests. He faces them, like Abraham and like the ancient Israelites, in the wilderness. The way he responds to those tests reflects the responses of his predecessors. Each part of the Gospels' description of Jesus's testing draws from rich Jewish tradition and imagery. Understanding them will enrich the meaning and enhance the power of these familiar stories.

THE TEST OF SATAN

Jesus begins his testing in the wilderness at God's invitation. Jesus does not choose to be tested. Matthew 4 tells us that "the Spirit led Jesus up into the wilderness so that the devil might tempt him" (Matthew 4:1). This invitation echoes the Old Testament text in which we first meet Satan. That text is the Book of Job. The context of Job differs slightly, but the similarities are instructive. The primary similarity is that God initiates the test. Even though Satan prods God, it is God who chooses to test Job. While Satan does not prod God in Matthew, God is the one who initiates the test.

In assigning the primary testing role to God, both Job and Matthew reflect the testing of Abraham in Genesis. These similarities suggest that God uses tests to determine loyalty. This usage reflects the meaning of faith in biblical Judaism. Faith is not principally a matter of believing certain truths or ideas. Faith is loyalty. Faith is following God. The Hebrew word often translated as faith—*emunah*—actually means "faithfulness." We express our faith through faithfulness to God's commandments. Thus, a test of faith is not simply a matter of asking people whether they believe in one thing or another. It is about seeing whether they remain faithful to God's commandments.

The primary difference between Matthew and Job is also instructive. In Job, it is God testing Job. In Matthew, it is God inviting Satan to test Jesus.

What would it feel like if I and others truly forgave those who hurt us?

Put differently, in Job, God tests man. In Matthew, God tests God through Jesus. The reason for this difference lies in the purpose of each test. The purpose of Job is to teach the meaning of *emunah*, of faithfulness. In Matthew, it is to show God's power over Satan. It is also, as we will see, to connect Jesus with the Jewish patriarchs and ancient Israelites.

WHY THE WILDERNESS?

The first connection lies in the location of the test. The wilderness is away from all distractions. It is unclaimed territory. A person can choose his or her loyalties in the wilderness, and those loyalties matter because the wilderness is a place that reveals our dependency. We cannot survive without support. We cannot survive alone. Thus, in the Book of Exodus, the Israelites are tested in the Sinai wilderness, and it is there that they pledge their loyalty to God.

The way in which they express their loyalty reveals the risk they took. According to the Jewish sages, they accepted the Law given by God to Moses without knowing its contents. The sages teach that God invited different peoples into the wilderness and asked them if they would accept the Law. These peoples asked what was in it. When God responded by reciting the Ten Commandments, each group of people and their leaders rejected the Law. They said they could not abide by it. When God came to the Israelites and asked them if they would accept the Law, they said yes. They did not even ask about its contents. In the wilderness they proclaimed their ultimate allegiance to God. Their faithfulness, like that of Abraham, came without question and with utter devotion.

Jesus follows this example. He is in a place of utter dependence on God. As the text tells us, Jesus fasted in the wilderness for forty days and forty nights. The literal truth of this statement is less important than the teaching it conveys. In Judaism fasting symbolizes sacrifice. It was a way of giving something up as a sign of gratitude to and dependence on God. In the Talmud the rabbis compare afflicting one's body via fasting to offering an animal as a sacrifice on the altar at the Jerusalem Temple. Both require us to give up something important.

Fasting also serves to bring a person into a particular state of mind. Today we might call it light-headed. When we fast, our minds do not process the world around us in the same way they do when we are satiated. This light-headedness might serve to make us more open to spiritual discernment or transformative experiences. That it is not to say faith requires us to be light-headed. It simply means that not eating can bring about a state of mind that opens us up to extraordinary experiences.

Most Jews today, for example, fast on the holy day of Yom Kippur. Yom Kippur means "Day of Atonement." Part of the reason is to give up something important to us so we feel gratitude for what God has given us throughout the year. I have experienced, however, the other reason for fasting as well: a heightened spiritual awareness that makes us more open to God's reality. It happened near the end of the day during the concluding worship service. The prayer we were chanting spoke of the Gates of Heaven and the way God opened them especially wide on Yom Kippur. We entered those gates through forgiveness. Hungry and light-headed, I found that the image of those gates felt especially compelling, and I imagined what it would feel like if I and others truly forgave those who hurt us. A different world appeared possible. It was an unexpected nonrational (though not irrational) spiritual experience, and the combination of fasting and prayer made it possible.

The reason we need not take the forty days of fasting literally is that we know this is a trope from the Old Testament. In the Book of Exodus, Moses fasts as he spends forty days and forty nights atop Mount Sinai. Even before that, Genesis tells us the flood during Noah's time lasted forty days and forty nights. After leaving the Egypt of his childhood, Moses spent forty years in the land of Midian. Forty symbolizes a period of testing. If a person can survive forty days in a certain condition, his or her faith can be trusted. His or her faith has been confirmed. This theology helps us understand why God is so angry with the Israelites when they build a golden calf during the time Moses was atop Mount Sinai. Their trust in God could not last the whole forty days. They needed a replacement. It is only through Moses's intervention that they survive.

If this notion of a probationary period during which a faith is tested seems strange, consider the ways we do it today. When people enter the military, they have to survive a seven-week boot camp. The period is essentially a probationary time when they need to prove their fitness for the service. Or consider people who enter new jobs. They often need to prove themselves for a period of time before they can feel secure in the position. Sometimes we think of faith as an instantaneous all-or-nothing decision. But the Bible understands it as a process. It requires patience and persistence. It requires a sacrifice. It does not come quickly or easily. That is why Matthew emphasizes the forty days and forty nights of Jesus's fasting. His spiritual strength is so vast that even as he is starving in the wilderness, he resists Satan's temptation.

THE JEWISH UNDERSTANDING OF SATAN

Devil is derived from a Greek word meaning "slanderer" or "accuser." The precise nature of the devil—Is he a force totally separate from God? Does he have a proper name? Is he a fallen angel—varies in different Christian theologies and denominations. The Jewish environment in which Jesus lived, however, had a clear understanding of the meaning of the devil. The devil is an adversarial force who *tests God*. The name for this force is *HaSatan*, which in Hebrew means "the Adversary." Thus, Satan is not a proper name. It refers to a being—probably some sort of angel, as we read in Numbers 22:22—who challenges and tests God. The most prominent example of this usage in the Hebrew Bible is in the Book of Job, where we read of *HaSatan* questioning whether the human being Job is really that faithful to God. Indirectly, *HaSatan* is questioning whether God really has the power to demand and sustain the faith of human beings. Thus, while it seems *HaSatan* is challenging Job, he is really challenging God.

Why would the Old Testament depict an angel serving as God's *Satan*, God's adversary? The sages in the Talmud offer a compelling answer to this question. They suggest that the angels were suspicious of human beings from the moment God decided to create them. The Talmud tells a story of God gathering with His angels and announcing His plans to create human beings. The angels are stunned. "Don't you realize human beings will bring violence and mayhem in your world? Don't you know they will betray you?" the angels ask God. God hesitates. Then, however, God decides human beings are worth the risk. God creates them over the angels' protests.[1]

The Talmud does not go on to speak of a fallen angel, though some Jewish texts during the time of Jesus do. The Jewish texts of the first century that do speak of a fallen angel connect their view with a verse from the biblical Book of Isaiah, which reads,

> How you are fallen from heaven,
>   O Day Star, son of Dawn!
> How you are cut down to the ground,
>   you who laid the nations low!
> (14:12-14, my translation)

They are generally apocalyptic in tone. The more mainstream first-century Jewish views see Satan in both spiritual and physical terms. Professor Hershey Friedman summarizes these different views in an article about Satan in Jewish literature, writing, "Satan is often identified as a person's evil inclination in Jewish thought—an internal counterbalance to one's good inclination, both of which are under a person's control. Satan is also the Angel of Death, an angel whose duty is to take the souls of individuals whose time has come."[2] Finally, Satan is the angel who tests individuals, tempts them into sin, and then testifies against them in the heavenly tribunal, hence the name "accuser." Behind all of these interpretations is the understanding that the angels are subordinate to God. As we have seen, God creates human beings despite the angels' vociferous opposition. Keep these Jewish understandings of Satan in mind as we explore the temptations Jesus faces in the wilderness.

THE THREE TEMPTATIONS

The first temptation—Satan's invitation for Jesus to turn stones into bread—would have immediately reminded first-century Jews of God's commanding Moses to speak to a stone in order to produce water. This story is told in Numbers 20. Moses responds by striking the stone rather than speaking to it, and this act was considered disobedient because it suggested Moses himself rather than God produced the water. God punishes Moses for this disobedience by not allowing him to enter the Promised Land.

Although Jesus's temptation differs from that of Moses, it emerges out of a similar need. He is hungry, and Satan is tempting him with the opportunity to eat bread. Jesus's response quotes Moses from Deuteronomy saying man does not survive by bread alone. The linkage here between Jesus and Moses is deliberate and powerful. It presents Jesus as both similar and superior to Moses. Both faced temptation, yet Jesus passed and Moses failed. As a result, Moses dies outside the Promised Land whereas Jesus returns to and dies within it.

The next test moves beyond Moses to echo a different period in Jewish history. Here Satan invites Jesus to ascend to the top of the Temple in Jerusalem and throw himself down. If he truly is the son of God, Satan says, he has nothing to fear. God will save him. Jesus declines, once again quoting the Book of Deuteronomy. This time it is Deuteronomy 6:16, "Don't test the LORD your God the way you frustrated him at Massah." Massah is a location in the Sinai wilderness where the Israelites complained bitterly to Moses about the lack of water. They complained that Moses took them out of Egypt, where they may have been slaves but at least had food and drink. Now they have nothing. The incident is described in Exodus 17:1-7.

The Hebrew word *Massah* means "test." In complaining about their lack of water, the Israelites seem to be criticizing Moses. Yet, in response, Moses says "Why are you testing the LORD?" (Exodus 17:2). The Bible understands the Israelites' complaints as signaling a lack of faith. They did not trust that

God would assuage their thirst and save their lives. By complaining to Moses, they were testing God. They were asking whether God could truly provide for their needs. In criticizing this behavior, the Bible is conveying a lesson. While God may test humans, humans should not test God.

The second temptation echoes this lesson. Satan is inviting Jesus to express a similar lack of faith—and to test God as the Israelites did. By quoting Moses's words from Deuteronomy, Jesus signals both his faith and similarity with Moses. It is not wise to test God. The text from Deuteronomy is also an apt one because of what follows it. The next verse from Deuteronomy emphasizes the importance of obedience and the promises that obedience will serve as a protection from death and destruction. In other words, Jesus illustrates trust in God by following God's commandments, not in daring God through outrageous acts.

The final test also echoes the book of Deuteronomy. Satan brings Jesus to the top of a high mountain and shows him all the kingdoms of the world. Satan promises Jesus earthly power over them if he abandons God and worships him. Jesus declines, turns Satan away, and quotes Deuteronomy 6:13, "You will worship the Lord your God and serve only him" (Matthew 4:10).

God is eternal and unchangeable. But the way we relate to God evolves over time. The God we pictured when we were four differs from the God we picture when we are forty.

Right away, the language and imagery would remind first-century Jewish listeners of the final scene of Moses's life. He is standing atop a high mountain. God invites him to look out. Yet, God only invites him to see the land of Canaan. God is not testing Moses, though one could argue that Moses could have tried to run into the land of Canaan and violate God's admonition that he could not enter it. What is striking, though, are the differences we see between this scene in Deuteronomy and the text from Matthew. In Matthew, it is Satan who invites Jesus to look down from a high mountain. And Satan shows him not only the land of Canaan, but all the kingdoms of the world. In addition to showing Jesus's power to resist temptation, Matthew may also be signaling Jesus's singular importance in comparison to Moses. Whereas Moses cannot enter the Promised Land, Jesus is able to return to it. While Moses simply receives the Torah, Jesus becomes the embodiment of the Torah. As Professors Amy-Jill Levine and Marc Brettler put it, "Jesus is shown all the kingdoms of the world, but Moses is shown only Canaan . . . whereas Moses leads the people to their earthly home; Jesus leads followers to the kingdom of heaven. Moses receives the Torah from God and gives it to Israel; Jesus is the fulfillment of Torah as well as its authoritative interpreter."[3] In other words, Jesus is not just like Moses but also, as Matthew suggests, superior to him.

THE ONGOING POWER OF THE BOOK OF DEUTERONOMY

Matthew is clearly aware of the Jewish world in which Jesus lives. His writing draws from and responds to it. It is no accident that Jesus continually quotes from the Book of Deuteronomy. He quotes Deuteronomy more than any other biblical book. Why? Deuteronomy expresses a Judaism more modern and universalist than other parts of the Torah. It forms the basis for rabbinic Judaism, the milieu in which Jesus lived and taught—and it is especially relevant for Christians today.

This came home to me during a year I spent studying Deuteronomy with a local Christian minister friend. We had talked about studying together, and he suggested Deuteronomy. The study expanded us both. While we differ in our view of the Old Testament, we both came to see Deuteronomy as strikingly modern. Jesus continually quotes it for a reason.

First, the God it describes is accessible and universal. God is eternal and unchangeable. But the way we relate to God evolves over time. The God we pictured when we were four, for example, differs from the God we picture when we are forty. In the Book of Exodus, God inflicts ten horrendous plagues on Egypt. In the Book of Leviticus God enjoys the smell of the animal sacrifices offered by the Israelites. In Deuteronomy, however, God is not described in such dramatic action and sensory detail. God, rather, is a presence, a force for justice, whose word is revealed through the prophet Moses. God is much closer to the "still, small voice" later heard by the prophet Elijah. God is much closer to the presence we feel today.

Second, the moral vision Deuteronomy presents challenges and enlarges us because the society it describes resembles, in many ways, our own. In the first four books of the Bible, the Israelites are a nomadic people. They are shepherds and herdsmen, resembling the few Bedouin groups that remain today.

Deuteronomy describes a more settled agricultural people. They farm and trade. They welcome immigrants from other countries. They have more sophisticated systems of social welfare. They have more centralized administrative structures. In other words, their society more closely resembles our own. Thus, the laws God reveals in Deuteronomy remain especially relevant. We remain concerned with immigration, knowing the Bible tells us not to oppress the stranger because we were strangers in the land of Egypt. We remain concerned with fair courts, remembering God's admonishing us never to take a bribe and or show undue favor to the poor or the rich.

Deuteronomy is also profoundly human. When Moses looks down into the Promised Land, tempted but knowing he cannot enter it, we can almost feel his pain. We can almost hear and see the tears rolling down his cheeks and feel the weightiness in his heart. Moses is a prophet, but he is also a human being with shortcomings and failures. He is not a perfect father. He is not a perfect husband. He does not live to see all his dreams fulfilled. Yet he lives a full life. He dies with "eyes undimmed" and "vigor unabated." He struggles to suck every morsel out of life. Like Moses and like Jesus, we will be tempted, we will be broken, but we can draw from our faith. We can struggle to live fully within the limitations God has given us.

ANGELS

As the temptations conclude, an angel appears to accompany Jesus out of the wilderness. This is the first angel we meet in the Gospels. Many modern Jews and Christians do not see angels as a part of Judaism. When I've spoken about angels to my congregation, I've gotten startled looks and people telling me Jews don't really believe in angels. They seem a vestige of fairy tales, of a bygone world.

Yet, a first-century Jew hearing this gospel would be intimately familiar with angels. He or she would know their role in Scripture and in Jewish tradition. A knowledgeable listener would likely have connected the angel in this story with the angel in God's most important test in the Old Testament: that is the test of Abraham in the Book of Genesis, where God commands Abraham to offer up his son, Isaac, as a sacrifice. That test is considered so important that it is recounted every year on one of Judaism's most sacred holiday, Rosh Hashanah, the New Year.

As in the temptations story, the angel appears at the end. And the angel plays a critical role. As Abraham lifts the knife and prepares to slaughter Isaac, the angel cries out and tells him to stop. The angel then affirms Abraham's faith, just as the angel affirms Jesus in Matthew. But this is only the beginning of the similarity. If we probe deeper into Jewish legend— into the part of Jewish literature known as *Midrash*—we see even more profound similarities. Midrash is a Jewish form of commentary and interpretation. The Hebrew word means "to explain." Midrash mainly fills in the gaps and tries to answer lingering questions in the Bible. Some parts of the Bible generate dozens of interpretations. None are necessarily the "correct" interpretation—they are all attempts to understand the meaning of the text and apply its lessons to daily life. The midrash was written over many centuries, and some forms of midrash continue to be written today. Those considered most authentic, however, were written in the first through fifth centuries.

Among them is one that explores the testing of Abraham. It suggests Satan accompanied Abraham and Isaac as they climbed Mount Moriah preparing for the sacrifice. Satan appears to Abraham in the guise of an old man. As they walk, Satan continually questions and harasses Abraham, suggesting he has lost his mind. He wonders why Abraham would agree to sacrifice his beloved son. He says God is trying to trick him and that the next day God will accuse Abraham of murdering his son. When Abraham does not give in, Satan starts placing physical obstacles in his path. Satan is trying to block him from reaching his destination. Once again it is to no avail.

Satan's approach here resembles his role in Matthew. He seeks to sow seeds of doubt in Abraham, inviting him to test God by not following his commandment. Satan is also playing on Abraham's weakness. Just as Satan knew Jesus was hungry from fasting and thereby tempted him with the dare to turn stone into bread, so Satan knows Abraham is anxious about God's commandment to sacrifice his son. What father wouldn't be? Abraham loves Isaac deeply. Isaac is the son he prayed for, the one who will continue the covenant. Satan is trying to turn Abraham's anxiety against him. First-century Jewish listeners would have recognized that technique in the Gospels. Even though the text does not go into great detail about it, we can imagine Jesus felt some anxiety. He was hungry. He was lonely. He did not know what was next on his journey. Satan gives him an appealing answer. Worship me, he says, and you will have power over all the kingdoms of the earth. Just as Abraham did, Jesus resisted. Satan fails to achieve his goal of forcing Abraham and Jesus to test God. And in both cases, an angel appears to celebrate and convey God's approval at the end.

Why does an angel appear rather than God? In Hebrew the word for angel is *malach*. The same Hebrew word also means "messenger." An angel is a messenger of God. Imagine this scenario: you are a student and your professor comes in to give you a test. He leaves the room and leaves you on your own to complete it. You struggle, you persist, you face great temptation—but you pass the test. Then when it's all over, the professor's chief assistant from the beginning comes in. She gives you a big hug and invites you to the next stage of your journey.

That's the way the angels work in Genesis and Matthew. They are God's messengers. God initiates the test. The angels bring Moses and Jesus to the next stage of their journeys. It is the next stage of our journey as well.

CHAPTER 5

CALLING THE DISCIPLES

The next stage of Jesus's journey would not be his alone. His test prepared him for spiritual leadership. But leaders need followers. For Jesus—as it was for other Jewish leaders of the time—followers were known as disciples. In fact, we would not know about Jesus had it not been for the disciples. Jesus did not write anything down. He did not leave archaeological artifacts for later scholars to discover. Rather, he left teachings for a group of people who eventually wrote them down and shared them with the world. It is fair to say that without disciples, we would not have Jesus. And if those disciples had not had disciples of their own, we would not know about them.

Who were these disciples? How did Jesus draw them in? Jewish tradition gives us a new way of looking at and answering this question. The entire rabbinic culture in which Jesus lived focused on the creation and training of disciples. Rabbi Yochanan Ben Zakkai, who founded rabbinic Judaism out of the ashes of the destruction of the Jerusalem Temple by the

Romans, knew that tradition dies without transmission from one generation to the next. A tradition needs to know how to make disciples. Jesus followed rabbinic tradition in making disciples, and the way his community operated resembled the way other rabbinic groups of the time did. Rabbi Jesus understood that a disciple is more than a follower. A disciple is more than a student. *A disciple is a link between the past, present, and future.* Without disciples we do not live on.

This is true not only in our spiritual lives but also in whatever is important to us. If we have an object important to us and we imagine it might become a family heirloom, how do we ensure it remains? We teach our children or grandchildren to value it. If we have a family custom that is important, how do we ensure that it continues? We bring the next generation into the practice so that they can sustain it. Jesus does something very human in cultivating disciples. And seeing the way he does so not only enriches our understanding of the Bible, it gives us insight into how we can ensure the survival of what is most sacred to us.

Rabbis like Jesus worked to find disciples with what the Jewish sages called ruach Elohim, *the spirit of God.*

THE MAKING OF DISCIPLES

How does Jesus make disciples? What causes Mark, Peter, and others to follow him? The Bible itself is tantalizingly vague. Jesus simply says, "Come follow me, and I will send you out to fish for people." That's it. Fortunately, we have ample evidence of how discipleship worked in first-century Jewish life. Rabbis like Jesus worked to find disciples. They looked for certain qualities of character. They did not seek simply the strongest or most intelligent. They sought disciples who could become leaders. They sought not to create followers but to build up new leaders. They also sought those imbued with what the Jewish sages called *ruach Elohim*, the spirit of God. This spirit is difficult to define, but it generally referred to a commitment to the religious acts of study and prayer. Sometimes disciples would even undergo a kind of test or probationary period, where they would study in a rabbi's school to see if they still wanted to become a disciple.

The rabbi-disciple relationship was not a one-way street. Disciples also had expectations of their master. Nothing was off-limits. The master's public and private lives were open for the disciples to study. The master also had to respect the disciples. Jewish texts suggest the rabbi often learned much from his disciples. The master had to teach through word and deed. His character needed to be consistent in public and private. One story in the Talmud tells of a master teacher who became disqualified when his "inside did not match his outside." In other words, his behavior undermined the values he sought to teach. Too much pride and unethical acts compromised his ability to teach his disciples. Disciples had high expectations of their rabbis.

In looking at Jesus's call to the disciples, we are going to read between the lines of the text. We are going to ask how his disciples looked at Jesus and understood his actions. We are going to explore why Peter and others followed him. And we will search for the clues that can lead us to become better disciples, teachers, and leaders ourselves.

A SACRED PURPOSE

The first biblical disciple was Abraham. When he answered God's call to leave his homeland and go to the Promised Land, he effectively became God's disciple. What lured Abraham? What drew him to God? It was a sacred purpose. It was a mission. God promised Abraham that all the world would be blessed through him (Genesis 16). Those whom he blessed and who blessed him would prosper. From that moment on, Abraham was on a mission from God.

Jesus also offers his disciples a sacred purpose. He says, "I will make you become fishers of men" (Mark 1:17 NKJV). They would move from physical fishing to spiritual fishing. Their talents would serve a sacred purpose. Jesus appeals to their higher selves. The psychologist Abraham Maslow spoke of the levels of human development. At the bottom are the need for food and shelter. That is where the fishermen are operating when Jesus meets them. According to Maslow, we move up the hierarchy until we reach a sense of personal mission or purpose. We recognize that we are much more than physical beings. We can do more than meet our own physical needs. Jesus invites the disciples to join him and reach that level.

A good master also realizes his disciples' unique gifts. Jesus knows that someone who has patience to catch fish may also have the patience and character to develop spiritual followers. A parallel story of discipleship in the Talmud illustrates the way this process worked. It also takes place in the water. Instead of the Sea of Galilee, however, it is set in the Jordan River.

A great rabbi named Yochanan was bathing in the river. He was spotted by a gang of thieves led by a man named Shimon

Ben Lakish (nicknamed Resh Lakish). Lakish believes he sees a beautiful woman in the river. He thrusts down his spear and jumps into the river. He grabs Yochanan, possibly intending rape. Yochanan responds by complimenting the marauder. He points out the great physical strength Lakish has, as evidenced by his jumping into the river, navigating its currents, and reaching him so quickly. Rabbi Yochanan says to Lakish, "Your strength should be used for Torah study." In other words, Yochanan suggests, instead of wasting your powers on robbery, use them to glorify God.

Lakish responds immediately to Yochanan with a compliment of his own. "Your handsomeness," he says to Yochanan, "should be used to seduce women." In other words, Lakish is saying Yochanan is wasting his good looks by focusing his energy on Torah study. Here we have a conflict of values. Yochanan symbolizes the spiritual. Lakish represents the physical. Yochanan, however, devises a plan to win over Lakish. He says, "If you repent of your evil ways and bring your strength to study, I will give you my beautiful sister as a wife." While this offer may offend our modern sensibilities, it does appeal to Lakish. He agrees and leaves with Yochanan to devote his life to study. He becomes Yochanan's greatest disciple, and one of the most cited rabbis in the Talmud. Yochanan recognized his gift, and taught him to use it to serve God.[1]

STUDY AND SUDDENNESS

Both Resh Lakish and the early disciples of Jesus make a split decision. They are invited to become disciples, and they accept without hesitation. If this quickness seems strange or foolhardy, consider the important decisions you have made in your life. Did you ever instantly feel you needed to pursue a certain relationship or follow a particular calling? Having officiated at over three hundred weddings, I can say that, quite often, one of the partners will say that he or she felt they would marry their partner soon after meeting them. As Malcolm Gladwell showed in his wonderful book *Blink*, some of the most critical decisions in life are made in an instant.[2]

Even so, choosing to become a disciple was a momentous decision. It involved leaving behind one's previous way of life, as with Resh Lakish, and even one's family of origin. Becoming a disciple meant embracing a new way of life. We see this truth in the very word itself. A disciple lives by a new discipline. This discipline—this rhythm and way of living—does not just apply to prayer or study. It applies to one's entire life. I remember learning this from a rabbinic mentor who told me that becoming a rabbi is not simply a job. It is a way of life. The Hebrew word for disciple—like the identifier used to refer to Jesus's—is *talmid*. A *talmid* is a student. *Talmids* are students of their master's way of life. They learn from everything their master does.

To illustrate this truth, the Jewish sages would often use extreme examples. One of them is found in the Talmud in a story about Rabbi Meir and one of his more earnest disciples. Rabbi Meir was in his bedroom with his wife. They were about to become intimate with each other when they heard a strange sound. Rabbi Meir looked under the bed and found his disciple lying underneath it. An infuriated Meir asked the disciple what he was doing there. The disciple answered, "This, too, is Torah. And I must understand it."

There is something humorous about this story, of course, but the story also hints at the deeper meaning of discipleship. It was all-encompassing. The notion of privacy as we understand it today did not apply to the master-disciple relationship. The trust and transparency was total. Disciples were expected to imitate their master's actions. Consider John 13:13-15, where Jesus teaches the disciples to wash others' feet just as he washes theirs. Jesus teaches his disciples a countercultural worldview, and they embrace it. They trust him as he overturns the established order.

Once again the model for this trust was Abraham. As noted earlier, when he answers God's call, Abraham becomes the first Jewish disciple. The Bible clearly indicates that Abraham was making a radical break with the past. God tells him to leave his father's house and journey to the land that God will show him. He is to leave all that is familiar and normal to him and travel to a place that must have seemed as though it were on the other side of the world. It is not simply a physical journey. Abraham's father's house symbolizes the world in which Abraham lived. It represents the status quo governed by different gods. The one God of the universe is inviting Abraham to leave this world behind. God is inviting Abraham to follow Him in creating a new order based, as a later rabbi would say, on the vision of "one God over all, and one human family of all."

HOW DID JESUS TEACH HIS DISCIPLES?

As a rabbi, the essential thing that Jesus did was *teach*. Rabbis gathered disciples, taught them, and spread their religious message to their community. During the next century the term *rabbi* began to convey a more formal educational process and status. A rabbi studied at a school for a prescribed period of time and then was formally designated a rabbi by another rabbi. It became a formal title rather than a functional one. During Jesus's life, however, it was a functional one, and Jesus served in that function.

Rabbis had a distinct teaching style. It relied on questions and stories. A rabbi taught by asking questions and then questioning the answers given by students. The questions and answers would continue until an issue was resolved, although sometimes a debate would end with multiple answers. Stories were often interspersed within the questions and answers. A wonderful example begins the book of Jewish law, the *Mishnah*. The Mishnah was completed around 100 CE, but it gathered oral teachings that had been part of Jewish life for centuries.

The Mishnah begins with a question. At what time is it permissible to recite the evening Shema? (The Shema is a prayer said three times a day: morning, noon, and night. We will come back to this prayer in chapter 8.) The students discussing this text would have known that they are obligated to say the Shema three times a day. What they don't know is when evening officially begins and ends. They begin to debate. One group says the evening Shema has to be said during the time a person gets ready to go to sleep. Another group says a person can say it anywhere from sunset to midnight. Another rabbi says one can say the evening Shema up until dawn of the next day.

To prove this last answer, one of the rabbi relates a story about a great rabbi of an earlier generation whose sons returned late from a wedding party. He told his father he had not yet said the evening Shema. The rabbi told him he could say it up until dawn. Thus, if that great rabbi had permitted the saying of the evening Shema until dawn, so should they. Ultimately, after even further debate, the rabbis conclude that the evening Shema should be said by midnight, but in extraordinary circumstances, it can be recited until dawn.[3]

Jesus followed this practice and frequently taught with questions. As Reverend Martin Copenhaver points out in his book *Jesus Is the Question*, Jesus asks 307 questions, and he only answers three of them.[4] Much like the rabbis, the disciples learned through debating the answers to those questions. This technique of using questions to teach was new in first-century Jewish life. The Israelite prophets issued proclamations with occasional rhetorical questions. They declared rather than questioned. The rabbis, however, questioned in order to discern. The process of answering the question was more important than arriving at a precise right answer.

Jesus did differ from the rabbis in that he asked more open-ended questions. The rabbis, for example, did not ask their disciples questions like "Where is your faith?" which Luke has Jesus asking the disciples, or "Why are you afraid? Have you still no faith?" which Mark records (Luke 8:25; Mark 4:40, my translation). This difference may reflect Jesus's unique style and focus. They also reflect the mysticism we see in the Gospels, especially in John the Baptist. The rabbis thought and taught in a more legal framework.

Jews are part of a story that began with Abraham. So are Christians.

Questions were key to Jesus's teaching style, and so were stories—especially parables. Parables (stories told to illustrate a lesson or truth) were a hallmark of rabbinic pedagogy—scholars estimate rabbinic literature contains about 3,500 parables. Rabbis relied so heavily on parables in part because rabbis taught orally. Few texts were written down until the second or third century. Thus, a teaching had to be easy to remember and convey to others. Parables are also subject to multiple interpretations, allowing them to speak to people in different life circumstances. They are also occasionally enigmatic. We find ourselves thinking about them even after we have heard them many times.

We even have a parable about why parables work. This parable has two characters: Truth and Story. It begins with Truth walking down the street, looking depressed and forlorn. His clothes are tattered, and his face looks worn. He runs into his friend Story. Story is dressed in the finest clothes. He has a big smile on his face. Story asks his friend what's wrong. Truth tells him he's depressed and alone. Nobody believes what he says. Story tells him the problem is not in the content of what he says. It is in the way he says it. "If you took the time to dress as I do," Story tells him, "you would find many friends who would listen to you. If you simply appear the way you are, no one will listen." Story opens up a path in our hearts and minds for Truth.

The rabbis realized this and taught Truth with Story. So did Jesus. I bet you do as well. How do you convey important family lessons? You probably tell a story about them. When our family gets together for Passover, for example, we always tell the story about my grandfather returning from Europe after the Second World War and celebrating Passover with his new bride, parents, and siblings. This story makes our family gathering more meaningful. How do you convey what is important to you? In addition to actions, you probably use stories. Stories help us make sense of the world. They make the abstract real. My children, for example, recently asked my wife and me what it means to be in love and to be married. We told them the story of how we met (in the library at seminary), the places we visited, the dates we shared, and then what happened at our wedding. The stories helped our children understand the meaning of love and marriage.

Stories also help us understand ourselves. They help us see our lives as eternally significant. When our lives are part of a story, we can see part of us living before and after our own time on this earth. Jews are part of a story that began with Abraham. So are Christians, and that story includes Jesus at the cross. Every individual, in fact, is part of a story.

In a recent book about the secrets of happy families, Bruce Feiler suggests that exploring our stories makes us happier and healthier. Scientists discovered this by asking children a series of questions. They included: Do you know where your grandparents grew up? Do you know where your mom and dad went to high school? Do you know where your parents met? Do you know an illness or something really terrible that happened in your family? Do you know the story of your birth? When the children knew the answers to these questions, they had a much greater likelihood of thriving and coping with difficult circumstances. They felt greater control over their lives. They were even more resilient after 9/11. They had what Feiler calls an "intergenerational self," finding meaning in seeing their own lives as part of a larger group and story. The rabbis—including Rabbi Jesus—helped disciples find their sacred selves. They were part of God's story, not just their own.[5]

SACRIFICE

The benefits of discipleship are now clear. Yet, we sometimes overlook the sacrifice required to become a disciple. What drew people to discipleship? We know that Resh Lakish was initially drawn to Yochanan's offer of his sister as a wife. The life Resh Lakish was leaving behind was not a terribly appealing one. He was a robber. We can understand, therefore, why he did not hesitate much in taking Yochanan up on his offer. Even Abraham was not leaving behind such a wonderful life. The Bible suggests his father was a wanderer, and later legend teaches he was an idol maker. Abraham had good reason to leave his old world behind.

How do we explain, however, the behavior of Peter and Andrew and then James and John? Aside from a sacred mission, Jesus does not seem to offer them any worldly gifts. They also had a healthy livelihood. They were not criminals. They were fishermen, a respectable and essential occupation in first-century Galilee. One could say they immediately sensed Jesus's divinity and were drawn by his truth and charisma. The text, however, does not give us any indication of this. When they decide to follow Jesus, they are making a tremendous sacrifice. Becoming a disciple was not a self-evident path. It was a choice to give up a comfortable life and risk a journey to the unknown.

Was this common among Jewish disciples in the first century? The answer seems to be yes. One of the apostle Paul's

Calling the Disciples

contemporaries was a rabbi named Akiba. Akiba was a peasant and a poor shepherd. At age forty, he encountered a neighbor named Eliezer Ben Hyrcanos. Eliezer was a famous rabbi, and he invited Akiba to study with him. According to the Talmud, Akiba lived in abject poverty for twelve years while studying. In one story he and his wife own only a bed of hay on which they sleep. Yet, when a beggar comes seeking a place to sleep, they give him half of the bed. Akiba persists in his studies and becomes the greatest sage of his era.

Akiba, like Yochanan and Resh Lakish, devoted himself to study. Study was a means of worship. It also demanded sacrifice because the Romans sought to stamp it out. Akiba told a famous story about the rabbinic response to Roman persecution. A Roman soldier asked him why he would not give up study of Torah. It had become forbidden by Roman law, and Akiba and his students had to study in secret. Akiba answered by asking why a fish being chased by a larger fish would not just leave the water and come onto the land. A fish cannot live without water just as a Jew and Judaism cannot live without Torah.

THE KINGDOM OF HEAVEN

Akiba and his disciples sacrificed themselves for the study of Torah. This sacrifice highlights both a similarity and difference between Jewish disciples of Akiba and those of Jesus. The disciples of Jesus sacrificed themselves for a belief in the realization of the kingdom of heaven. This phrase and idea is critical in understanding discipleship, Jesus, and the Gospels. It is also deeply rooted in rabbinic Judaism.

Kingdom of heaven really means kingdom of God. As Professor David Flusser has pointed out, "'Heaven' is a circumlocution for 'God,' and people in general believed that when the kingdom of God came, Israel would be freed from the yoke of Rome."[6] Using *heaven* and *God* interchangeably is characteristic of rabbinic Judaism as well, where we often read about "arguments for the sake of heaven," which were debates to try to figure out what God truly wants or intends of us.

In hearing the phrase "kingdom of heaven," a first-century Jew would have heard echoes of the phrase "Day of the Lord," which is frequently mentioned by the Hebrew prophets. The Day of the Lord was judgment day. It was one where people were separated on the basis of righteousness and devotion to God's laws. It was the end of days, an apocalyptic replacement of earthly rule by divine sovereignty. The precursor to this day would be the arrival of the "son of man," or the "messiah," as noted in the Book of Daniel and throughout the Gospels.

Rabbinic Judaism also held that the kingdom of heaven was not imminent. It was possible, but it depended on total devotion to God's laws. When Jews follow God's laws only, they will bring about the kingdom of heaven. Until then they would have to survive under Roman rule. In fact, rabbinic theology held that foreign powers like Rome served as God's way of punishing the Jewish people for not committing themselves to God's laws. In other words, the Romans were not threatening God. They were doing God's will by punishing Israel for its lack of faith.

Jesus drew from rabbinic Judaism's emphasis on the human role in realizing the kingdom of heaven. It was up to the people to follow God's law. That was one of the prerequisites for the coming of the kingdom. But Jesus also drew from another strand of Jewish thought—that of the Essenes and the Dead Sea sect. They foresaw a radical break with the earthly kingdom and the kingdom of heaven. The kingdom of heaven was not something that could be brought about by human action or initiative. It was a divine decision. It would involve cosmic struggle between God and Satan, between the Princes of Light and Darkness.

Glimpses of this apocalyptic point of view can be found throughout the Christian Bible. It is found most prominently in the Revelation, but it also appears in the Gospels. Its adherents believed the kingdom of heaven was imminent. John the Baptist emphasizes this view repeatedly, saying, "the shovel [God] uses to sift the wheat from the husks is in his hands. He will clean out his threshing area and bring the wheat into his barn. But he will burn the husks with a fire that can't be put out" (Matthew 3:12; Luke 3:17). For followers of John the Baptist—and for the group of rebellious Jews known as Zealots—the chaff was Rome. God would destroy Rome fully and quickly, ushering in the kingdom of heaven.

Jesus draws from both the rabbinical and apocalyptic views in articulating a unique concept of the kingdom of heaven. He draws from the rabbinic view in emphasizing the human role in bringing about the kingdom. Realization of the kingdom demands repentance or what the rabbis called *teshuvah*, the Hebrew word for "return." We see this view in Matthew where Jesus says to his disciples, "Repent, for the kingdom of heaven is at hand" (4:17 NKJV). These words are not meant to serve as a warning. Jesus is not saying, "You need to repent or you will get left behind because the kingdom of heaven is about to arrive." Rather, Jesus is following the rabbinic idea that through repentance, prayer, and acts of charity, human beings can bring about the kingdom of heaven.

Jesus does believe, however, in contrast to the rabbis, that *Jews of the first century are closer to the kingdom of heaven than they have ever been.* He believes the community occupies a middle ground between earlier human history and the end of days. The kingdom of heaven was a possibility for those who chose to enter it. As David Flusser puts it, "Jesus is the only Jew of ancient times known to us who preached not only that people were on the threshold of the end of time, but that the new age of salvation had already begun. This new age had begun with John the Baptist who made the great break-through."[7] Jesus departs from rabbinic Judaism in seeing the kingdom of heaven as not only a historical event but also a spiritual possibility.

The disciples are the ones who carry on and emphasize that spiritual possibility after Jesus's death. We would not know anything about him had the disciples not done so. The disciples were also precious to Jesus because they were his first followers. As we will see in the next chapter, Jesus soon gained many more followers. His fame and message began to spread, transforming the land of Israel and the Jewish people.

CHAPTER 6

DO YOU BELIEVE
IN MIRACLES?

I f you look at leading politicians, celebrities, or athletes, you often see that their closest friends and confidants are the people they knew before they became rich or famous. Think of President Obama and his senior advisor, Valerie Jarrett, or basketball star Lebron James and his small circle of close friends from high school. A person who becomes extremely powerful or wealthy attracts people who want something from him or her. It becomes difficult to make new friends when you are unsure of their motives. Do they want something you can give them, or is it a genuinely mutual relationship?

I think the Bible was aware of this phenomenon, and so was Jesus. The disciples to whom he was closest joined him before he performed any miracles. They became his friends before he became widely known. Jesus knew these disciples would not be fair-weather fans. They were genuinely committed to his ministry, even when it experienced its lowest points.

Thus, we should not be surprised that Jesus begins to perform miracles and healings only after the core disciples have joined him. These healings and miracles occur throughout his life, but they begin in earnest soon after the calling of the disciples.

Jesus is a rabbi, but he is a rebellious one.

The miracles have often been seen as a sign of Jesus's divinity. The Hebrew word for miracle implies a suspension of the natural order. Thus, a miracle is a supernatural event, and one who can perform the event has supernatural capabilities. Old Testament examples include the splitting of the Red Sea and the ten plagues. Some scholars and theologians see Jesus's miracles as part and parcel of this biblical tradition. He performs miracles in the Gospels in the same way God performed them in the Hebrew Bible. They serve as proof of his divine power. Believing in Jesus's miraculous powers is a core aspect of faith in him.

This view, however, does not reflect the understanding or role of miracles and healing in first-century Jewish life. Miracles were much more than a sign of supernatural power. They conveyed empathy. They relied on the spirit of the doer of miracles, not some external power given to them. Miracles and healing were not meant to impress. That is the way pagans understood miracles. Rather, miracles served as traces of God's presence in the world. Sometimes they violated the natural order. Other times they were simply unexpected occurrences.

In other words, first-century Jews understood miracles in much the same way we do. Sometimes they are extraordinary and mind-boggling: perhaps you know someone who beat a supposedly terminal cancer diagnosis. Surviving against the odds can be a miracle. Yet, miracles need not always be so extraordinary. Being forgiven can be a miracle. So can repairing a relationship. What unites these events is a sense of wonder. We say "it's a miracle" when something totally unexpected occurs. Such an event alters the way we look at the world. Many first-century Jews shared this view, and it offers us a new way of understanding and appreciating the miracles Jesus performs. Jews were not meant to see miracles as proof for or evidence of God. God does not need miracles to prove His existence. Rather, miracles happen for a purpose. They heal. They glorify. They teach. They also change perspective. Faith, I believe, is about discovering miracles in the everyday, not waiting every day for miracles to happen. We see this lesson when we examine Jesus's miracles through the lens of first-century Jewish life. And in so doing, we can learn how to see the miracles in our own lives.

THE EARLY MIRACLES

In the first chapter of Mark, we see Jesus perform several miracles. One of the first takes place in the synagogue in Capernaum, which is near the Sea of Galilee where Jesus found his first disciples. Jesus is teaching in the synagogue when a man begins screaming at him. The man says that Jesus is there to destroy them, although he also says that Jesus is "the holy one from God" (1:24). Jesus recognizes that the man is possessed by an evil spirit. This was a common affliction of the time. As we will soon see, the Talmud contains several stories of people possessed by an evil spirit. (Such spirits later came to be known as *dybbuks*—a Yiddish word meaning "demons"—

and were commonly mentioned in Jewish literature through the nineteenth century.) Jesus calls on the evil spirit to leave the man. It does. The story ends with people talking about Jesus's power and word spreading about him through the country.

An often overlooked part of the text hints at its deeper purpose. When the story begins, Jesus is teaching in the synagogue. The text tells us, "The people were amazed by his teaching, for he was teaching them with authority, not like the legal experts [or scribes]" (1:22). As we can infer, Jesus is already unpopular among the scribes. Scribes were the most conservative rabbinic scholars. The contrast here with the scribes reflects the larger tension between first-century Jewish miracle workers and the established rabbinic authority. Jesus is closer to the former. *He is a rabbi, but he is a rebellious one.*

He does not occupy this space alone. A possible contemporary of Jesus named Honi the Circlemaker is mentioned several times in the Talmud. Like Jesus, Honi lived in Upper Galilee, which was known for its disproportionate numbers of miracle workers. He was known as the Circlemaker because of an incident in which the land of Israel was experiencing a severe drought. People tried prayer. They tried offering more sacrifices. Nothing worked. Honi decided to draw a circle on the earth and stand in it until God brought forth rain. He stood in it and beseeched God. When it began to drizzle, Honi insisted on more and more. Soon he had to beg God to stop. And God did. This incident made him a legendary figure. The legends around Honi emphasized his special closeness to God. This closeness did not endear him to the Pharisees. After he produced the rain, the chief rabbi of the time, Simeon Ben Shatah, called him audacious. Yet, he also recognized his gift. The Talmud records Rabbi Simeon saying, "Were you not

Honi, I would excommunicate you. What can I do with you? You ingratiate yourself to God and He does what you ask, as when a son curries favor with his father, who then does what the son wants."[1]

Notice here the reference to Honi as a son of God. This is not meaning son in the same way the Gospels understand Jesus as the son of God, but it does provide a hint as to a source of the power of miracle workers. *It is rooted in relationship.* A miracle worker has an especially close relationship with God—like a father and son. This relationship gives him greater leeway than others. We see this in legends about Abraham, who is often referred to as God's friend. And we see a version of this model in King David, who is blessed with great success because he is beloved by God.

WHAT MAKES MIRACLES POSSIBLE?

Miracles are driven by the power of relationship. And relationships rely on faith. Our faith in another person—our trust in him or her—is the foundation of a relationship. That is why a marriage relies on faithfulness. That is why we can refer to someone as a "faithful friend." Faith creates relationships. And faith creates miracles. Honi's faith drove him to beseech God. So did Jesus's. And if we believe this kind of faith-powered miracle can't happen anymore, consider this Jewish legend. It is the story of a baker and a synagogue sexton. (A synagogue sexton is a combination of custodian, guard, and usher. A sexton typically live at the synagogue and work odd hours.)

The story takes place in a small town where the local baker was a regular at Sabbath worship. He was typically a bit bored, but one day the rabbi caught his attention. "In the ancient days of the Jerusalem Temple," the rabbi said, "twelve loaves of bread were prepared as an offering for God on every Sabbath. They were placed in the holiest place in the Temple."

This remark piqued the baker's interest. *I don't have time to attend Torah class. I'm not that interested in being on the Temple board*, he thought. *But I want to do something for the synagogue, and here's something I can do! I can make twelve extra loaves of bread each week and bring them to the temple and put them in the ark, the holiest place.*

So the next Friday morning, the baker did exactly what he had promised himself. He made twelve loaves of bread. He walked over to the synagogue. He went into the sanctuary and did just as the rabbi said the ancient priests had done in the Temple. He placed the twelve loaves in the ark and left the building with a smile on his face and pep to his step. He had fulfilled his responsibility.

A few minutes later, the sexton opened the sanctuary doors. He had his broom in hand, and he was sweeping the floor. After a moment, he paused and looked up. He began to pray. "God," he said, "You know I love working in your holy space. It is an honor to sweep the floors of this synagogue. But you know I have very little. I need a miracle. My children are hungry. Please help me."

Faith does not depend on miracles. Faith makes miracles possible.

A few minutes passed. Distracted by the intensity of his prayer, he didn't notice he was sweeping right in front of the ark. Suddenly he stopped. He was overwhelmed by the smell of freshly baked bread. He quickly opened the ark and found twelve piping-hot, fresh loaves!

"A miracle," he cried. It was enough to feed his family for a week. "Thank you, God," he proclaimed. And he, too, left the sanctuary with a smile on his face and a pep in his step. Truly, he understood, God performed miracles for those who believe.

The next morning, the baker was at Shabbat services. As the rabbi walked to the ark for the Torah service, the baker waited with bated breath. When the rabbi opened the ark, the baker gasped. The bread was gone. Words could not describe his joy. God had accepted his gift.

Next week, the baker returned to the temple. Again he placed the twelve loaves in the ark. Again he left with a joy-filled heart.

A few minutes later, the sexton walked with his broom into the sanctuary. He opened the ark, and the piping-hot bread greeted him. "This is truly miraculous," he proclaimed.

This pattern continued for several weeks. The baker would arrive and leave his bread. A few minutes later the sexton would open the ark and pick it up. Until the inevitable happened.

The baker was especially busy one Friday, and he arrived a few minutes later than usual. As he left his twelve loaves in the ark, the sexton walked in. He looked at the ark and caught the eye of the departing baker. Instantly they both knew what had been happening. There had been no miracles after all.

Or had there? It depends on our perspective. Perhaps miracles happen when we live by our highest values. Perhaps we open ourselves to miracles when we listen to a voice more sacred than our own. *Faith does not depend on miracles. Faith makes miracles possible.*

A MIRACLE OF HEALING

Following Jesus's miracle in Mark, he heals his disciple Simon's mother-in-law. This healing takes place on the Sabbath and is paralleled in the Gospel of Luke. Luke's account of the Sabbath healing is more extensive, making it a more fruitful source for examining Jesus's healing in its Jewish context.

The story begins with Jesus teaching in the synagogue. A woman who has been "disabled by a spirit" for eighteen years is in attendance, and when he sees her, Jesus calls to her and says "Woman, you are set free from your sickness." He places his hands on her, and she straightens up at once and praises God. This healing prompts the Pharisees in the synagogue to criticize Jesus for healing on the Sabbath. The story ends with the crowds rejoicing at Jesus's healing and the shame of his opponents.

On a simple, surface reading, this text has two purposes. First, it shows Jesus's miraculous healing powers, and second, it contrasts the kind Jesus with the legalistic Pharisees. A deeper reading, however, points to several unique and Jewish-rooted insights. The Pharisees were not opposed to healing. They did it themselves. And the Sabbath was not a time when life-transforming activities were forbidden. In fact, Sabbath worship includes a prayer for healing. Jewish law permits doctors to violate the Sabbath to address acute medical needs. Rather than contrast Jesus with the Pharisees, a deeper reading gives us new appreciation of the Pharisees and a recognition of Jesus's special concern for women.

The Pharisees understood healing power as a gift from God to those dedicated to His service. The Pharisees refer to the biblical prophets Elijah and Elisha as also having this power, which was passed down, like the Torah, to the Pharisees. In fact, Jesus heals in the same way Pharisees of the time did. To see this parallel, let us turn to a Talmudic story. It tells of a contemporary of Jesus and Honi, a Pharisee named Hanina Ben Dosa. He was known as a student of Rabbi Yochanan Ben Zakkai, who is credited with the founding of rabbinic Judaism after the destruction of the Jerusalem Temple. During his life, Hanina Ben Dosa was recognized for his power to exorcise evil spirits. One particular incident is relevant to our story. The incident begins with Rabbi Hanina immersing himself in a mikveh in a cave. This practice, as we learned in chapter 3, is an ancient Jewish ritual similar to baptism. The water purifies the person who immerses.

While Hanina is in the mikveh, a man wishing him harm places a rock over the cave opening. A spirit then comes and removes it. When Hanina arrives home, he is told that a woman in his neighborhood is suffering. He goes to her and finds she has been invaded by a spirit. He then says to the spirit, "Why do you cause grief to the daughter of Abraham?" The spirit answers him, "Is this how you repay me for removing the rock from the cave?" Hanina then orders the spirit to leave the woman's body. It complies.[2]

This odd story lends itself to several interpretations. The first is the ambivalent nature of the spirit. It both protects and harms. It protects Hanina but then harms the woman. Ultimately, it is subordinate to Hanina, who forces it out of the woman. When we look at its parallel with Jesus's healing, we see a striking similarity in language. Both Jesus and Hanina use the same words in describing the suffering woman. In Luke 13:16, Jesus says, "Then isn't it necessary that this woman, a *daughter of Abraham*, bound by Satan for eighteen long years, be set free from her bondage on the Sabbath day?" (emphasis mine). As we saw earlier, Hanina describes the woman afflicted with the spirit as a "daughter of Abraham."

This formulation, "daughter of Abraham," is striking. It appears rarely in Jewish texts and only in conjunction with healings. Jesus using it suggests he was familiar with Jewish healing customs. It also suggests Jesus's concern for women, who were, of course, among his earliest and most fervent followers. "Son of Abraham" is used much more often than "daughter of Abraham." In fact, she is the only woman in both the Old and New Testaments described as "daughter of Abraham." Had the healing been meant simply to demonstrate Jesus's miracle-working powers, the text would not have used this phrase. Perhaps the text means to tell us of Jesus's concern for women and his intention to make them more visible in Jewish life. The way in which the story is told also hints at this motivation. It is Jesus who calls out the woman. She does not approach him. Typically the sick person would come up seeking healing. Furthermore, the language is ambivalent on her malady. The Greek for "disabled by a spirit" could be understood as either physically or spiritually disabled. She may be crippled by her pain, feeling invisible to and ostracized by those around her. She would not likely have been the type of person to assert herself and approach Jesus to seek healing. Yet, when Jesus notices her—when he touches and calls her out—she is healed. By then referring to her as a "daughter of Abraham," Jesus is redefining her identity. A person who had been seen for eighteen years as disabled is now given rare and high praise.

THE REAL PURPOSE OF MIRACLES

Miracles today are often ridiculed. People who see religion as irrational and unscientific point to the miracles of the Bible and lampoon people who claim to believe them. This view is unfair to both God and people of faith. It seeks to define an entire tradition based on surface readings of complex stories. Yet, sometimes even those of us who advocate religion are guilty of misusing miracle claims. We assume everybody subscribes to our assumptions. We highlight some miracles and ignore others. And we suggest God performs miracles to prove His power. Sometimes it sounds as if we think God needs to perform grand miracles to convince people to take Him seriously. In other words, God is like a cosmic weight lifter. The bigger the miracle God does, the more we are impressed.

There are two serious problems if we subscribe to this understanding of miracles. The first is that miracles rarely lead to lasting faith. In the Hebrew Bible, for example, God performs signs and wonders—God splits the Red Sea—but three days later, the Israelites wish they were back in Egypt. They doubt God can provide them food in the wilderness. In the New Testament, Jesus's miracles frequently produce outrage and doubt among those around him. If we think miracles are meant to produce faith, we would have to conclude that they are not very successful tools. The greatest rabbi of the Middle Ages, Moses Maimonides, said there is always a danger in relying on miracles to prove one's faith because there is always the possibility they were the result of magic, optical illusion, or something similar.

The second problem is that the Bible does not lend itself to this view of miracles. The miracles were not intended to prove

God's power. Rather, they all had a role in advancing the story. Why did God split the Red Sea? Because the Israelites needed to cross it. Why did God bring down manna from heaven and water from a rock? Because the Israelites were hungry and thirsty. Had the purpose of the miracles simply been to show God's power, God could have performed a supernatural act with no other purpose than to demonstrate power. But God did not.

The same is true for Jesus's miracles. Why does Jesus perform miraculous healing? Because a sick person is in need. Why does Jesus walk on water? To calm the raging sea. The Jewish world in which Jesus lived and taught regarded miracles as a dangerous way to justify faith in God. We can believe in miracles, but we should not rely exclusively on them. Part of what makes God unique is that God does not need miracles to justify people's faith. As Jonathan Sacks put it,

> Miracles in the Bible are usually for the sake of impressing people who believe in that sort of thing. So the ten plagues and the division of the Red Sea are performed against the Egyptians. God sends fire at Elijah's request to defeat the false prophets of Baal. Even the appearance of God at Mount Sinai—with thunder, lightning and the sound of the ram's horn—is intended to awe a people who until a few weeks earlier had been slaves.[3]

Supernatural events serve a natural function. That function is not to prove God's power. The function is to teach us to heal, to pursue freedom, to feed those in need, and to challenge false and dangerous beliefs. Put differently, God teaches us how to live as human beings.

CAN YOU EXPERIENCE MIRACLES?

Those who write positively about miracles today fall into one of two camps. The first say miracles do happen. God does intervene in human life. We have to be mindful in assessing those claims. We need good evidence. But on occasion we can discern the divine hand literally shaping what happens on earth. The second camp says miracles are all a matter of perspective. They subscribe to an insight attributed to Albert Einstein: "There are only two ways to live your life. One is as though nothing is a miracle. The other is as though everything is a miracle." The problem with this formulation is that it takes God out of the miracle equation. From Einstein's point of view, miracles are totally subjective. They depend only on the perspective of the beholder. One person's miracle is another person's everyday occurrence.

I think Jewish tradition and wisdom provide us a third authentic way. Miracles do not depend on either a blind leap of faith or a subjective change in perspective. They flow from what Abraham Joshua Heschel called a "leap of action." We demonstrate God's power by behaving in godly ways. Believing is found in action rather than cognition, in what we do rather than what we profess. When we make a leap of action, we feel God's presence pushing us along. Miracles flow from that combination.

If you have ever seen the movie *Indiana Jones and the Last Crusade*, you'll know what I mean. In a seminal scene near the end, Indiana has to cross a vast chasm. He sees no bridge and has no rope. If he does not get to the other side, his father dies. His situation seems hopeless. He does not ask God to pick him up and bring him to the other side. He does not request a lightning bolt to heal his father. He simply takes one step into the chasm. As he does so, we see a bridge light up beneath his feet. The bridge had been there all along. He needed to take the first step in order to see it. He needed to take a leap of action.

A particular Jewish example of this view of miracles is found in the beloved holiday of Hanukkah. Ostensibly Hanukkah celebrates the supernatural miracle of a small jar of oil burning for eight nights. What should have lasted one night lasts for eight. God performs a miracle by causing the oil to burn for that long. But the eight nights of light was not the greatest miracle. *The greatest miracle was that the Jews who entered the temple and found the jar of oil decided to light it at all.* When they found the jar of oil, they knew it was miniscule. They knew it could not possibly last long enough for them to observe the eight-day holiday, which they had missed because they were in the midst of a war with the Assyrians. Yet, despite knowing their slim chances of success, they lit the first wick. They took a leap of action. They took the first step not knowing whether they would ever succeed in celebrating for all eight days. Had they not taken that step—had they not lit the first candle at all—we would have no eight days of miracles. We would have no Hanukkah. We would have no eight days of burning oil. Miracles do not cause faith. They arise from it.

Consider how this truth works in your own life. If you did not choose to enter into a relationship—with another person or with God—would you experience the beauty and the miracles that come out of it? If you did not go to a church or synagogue to pray, would you ever feel God's closeness or voice in your life? *Miracles depend on God, but they begin with us.* This truth has guided Jews and Christians throughout history. It helps explain how a story that began with a man named

Abraham and a woman named Sarah shapes the lives of billions of people today. It helps explain why a small, persecuted group known as Christians, who defined themselves as children of Abraham, grew into the largest faith in the world. They survived amid predictions of decline and irrelevance, spreading the message of Abraham throughout the world. Most faiths and peoples throughout history have disappeared from the world. The faith of Abraham survives. Can we call that a miracle? Absolutely. The miracle rests on our faith in God's teachings. Discovering those teachings—which Jesus lived and passed on to his disciples—brings us to chapter 7.

CHAPTER 7

FINDING HONEY
ON THE PAGE

In a traditional Jewish community, children receive their first Bible at age three. After they receive it, the rabbi asks them to open it to the first page. He or she then begins walking around the room and giving each child a dab of honey. As the students begin reading the text, they taste the honey, letting its sweetness linger in their mouths.

Why this strange ritual? Because God's words are sweet. Study is pleasurable. It is not like eating spinach and broccoli. It is like tasting the sweetness of honey on the tip of your tongue. The Book of Proverbs describes the Torah as a "tree of life." It nourishes us, planting us in the soil of tradition. Study nourishes that tree. The Torah is the strongest, sweetest nourishment we have.

Jesus likely began his Bible study in this traditional way. The Bible he studied was the Old Testament. He did not just memorize or repeat its verses. The ways he studied it were shaped by the methods and tools of a group of Jewish teachers known as the rabbis. The rabbis puzzled over, debated, and cherished each word. They filled in gaps with magnificent stories that sought to shed light on what God intended us to do or learn.

Jesus's teachings display all the hallmarks of rabbinic Judaism. Jesus interprets the biblical texts, he asks questions more than he offers answers, and he uses stories to illustrate deeper truths. In looking at the way Jesus teaches, we will explore examples of these rabbinic techniques. We will also see where some of the traditional contrasts between Jesus and Judaism—such as the abandonment of the dietary laws and the preference for love over law—have been overstated. Jesus did not depart significantly from rabbinic Judaism in understanding dietary practices. And Jesus did not seek to abandon the laws of the Old Testament or the Talmud in favor of grace and love. Rather, Jesus wove together strands of biblical and rabbinic Judaism in innovative ways that reflect the culture in which he lived. Seeing these innovations can help us appreciate the different strands in religious life today and offer us new questions to ask of our faith and ourselves.

OLD QUESTIONS, NEW ANSWERS

Text study is so interesting because texts are complicated and don't give easy answers. In fact, the more complicated the text, the more interesting it can be to study it (studying a complicated sonnet, for example, is more satisfying than studying a Hallmark greeting card verse). Sacred Scriptures are notoriously complex, which means that they invite a lifetime of study and also that people interpret the texts differently. Just as there are different schools of, say, Jane Austen scholarship, which each approach the study of Jane Austen novels with different assumptions and interests, two thousand years ago there were different schools of biblical interpretation. Specifically, Jewish interpreters of Scripture tended to fall into one of two schools of interpretation: the school of Rabbi Hillel and the school of Rabbi Shammai. Hillel and Shammai (and their students) were engaged in an internal debate about what it meant to be a good Jew. Responding to a rise in Roman persecution and the influence of Greek culture, they sought to define the core beliefs and practices of Judaism. Hillel typically looked for ways to adapt the law to people's needs and circumstances, while Shammai tended to offer strict and inflexible interpretations of biblical law. In legal terms, Hillel might be considered a more liberal constitutional scholar, whereas Shammai would be a strict constructionist.

HILLEL AND JESUS

Jesus most closely resembles Hillel in his Jewish teachings. To see how, compare Hillel's and Shammai's response to an outrageous request in a famous story—readers familiar with Jesus's teachings will hear that Jesus sounds a lot like Hillel. In this story a Roman man approaches both Hillel and Shammai and says to each of them, "Teach me the whole Torah while standing on one foot." Shammai is flabbergasted. He picks up a builder's rule, part of a two-by-four, and smacks the man on the head. The man walks away. He then approaches Hillel and makes the same outrageous request. Hillel answers, "That which is hateful to you, do not do to your fellow. That is the whole Torah; all the rest is commentary. Now go and learn it."

This story highlights a core difference between the two. Shammai had a strict approach to Jewish tradition. A Jew had to learn and follow all the laws and customs. A person seeking conversion to Judaism needed to learn and follow them. Shammai was also more pessimistic and cynical than Hillel. He saw Judaism's greatest glory in the past, in the days of King Solomon and the First Temple. People now, he said, had neither the knowledge nor the commitment of their forefathers. Their anger at the present circumstances of Jewish life led Shammai's followers to side with the Zealots in the war with the Romans. The Zealots believed in all-out confrontation and rejected any Jews who did not take their extreme position.

Love in Jewish tradition is not purely an emotion. It is also an active pursuit. It is a doing.

Hillel, on the other hand, embraced a more inclusive and conciliatory view of Judaism. Hillel opened up study of the Torah to anyone, not only to students deemed worthy, as was the case with Shammai. He was also optimistic, believing that Jewish life could survive and flourish even under Roman rule. Hillel and his disciples sought to reconcile with the Romans. They were initially rejected by the larger population in favor of the Zealots, but after the war concluded and the Temple was destroyed, their views gained influence. Much of the Talmud, in fact, reflects the point of view of Hillel. While Shammai's views are often recorded, Hillel's are usually accepted as the law. Hillel also abhorred violence and emphasized the possibility of forgiveness. We see this emphasis in his view of the death penalty. Capital punishment is permitted by Jewish law. Yet, Hillel said any court that inflicts death once every seventy years is considered a violent court. He did not reject the law of capital punishment. He simply did not enforce it.

We can immediately see the similarity between Hillel and Jesus when we look at one of the most memorable teachings in the Gospel. A Pharisee asks Jesus, "'Teacher, what is the greatest commandment in the Law?' He replied, 'You must love the Lord your God with all your heart, with all your being, and with all your mind. This is the first and greatest commandment. And the second is like it: You must love your neighbor as you love yourself. All the Law and the Prophets depend on these two commands'" (Matthew 22:36-40). Jesus could have responded by answering that they were all important. All the commandments are the word of God, thus all are critically important. Or Jesus could have said the law is secondary to the spirit. Don't bother yourselves with the law. Instead, Jesus, like Hillel, answers succinctly.

The first part of the answer quotes part of the Jewish prayer known as the Shema, which is found in the Book of Deuteronomy. (Jesus quotes more from the Book of Deuteronomy than any other book, as we have noted.) The first part of the Shema says, "Love your eternal God with all your heart, with all your soul, and with all your might." And then Jesus quotes Leviticus 19:18, "You must love your neighbor as yourself."

Love in Jewish tradition is not purely (or even primarily) an emotion. It is also an active pursuit. It is a doing. As one prominent Christian writer titled his recent book, *Love Does*. When Jesus quotes Deuteronomy and says, "Love the Lord your God with all your heart, with all your being, and with all your mind," he is not commanding a feeling. He is commanding action. In first-century Judaism, Jews demonstrated love for God through study, prayer, and deeds. Thus, Jesus says use your mind (study), use your body (deeds), and use your heart (prayer). Jesus is effectively summarizing Judaism in one sentence.

The second part of Jesus's answer speaks to our feelings rather than action. "Love your neighbor as yourself" was understood in Jewish tradition as emotive. It is not about action. It is about thought and feeling. In quoting this verse, Jesus is going further than Hillel did in answering the earlier question. Hillel said, "What is hateful to you do not do to another." Hillel is talking about refraining from certain actions. If you would not want someone to steal from you, for example, do not steal from someone else. Jesus, however, is talking about performing certain actions. If you want another person to turn the cheek if you struck him, for example, so should you. Jesus is not undermining the law. He is expanding the possibilities for fulfilling it. To do loving actions is a broader commandment than to refrain from hateful ones. It is an invitation to become part of the Jewish people by engaging in positive loving deeds. Seen in a Jewish context, Jesus's words in Matthew carve out a unique space in the Jewish debates of the time. While close to Hillel, Jesus is going further than Hillel in defining what it means to be Jewish. If one is willing to study and do loving deeds, Jesus is teaching, one can be Jewish.

THE ENDURING LESSONS OF HILLEL AND JESUS: PERSON OVER PROCEDURE

Debates rarely end with absolute victory by one point of view over another. Life is more complicated than black-and-white divisions. Within Judaism the school of Hillel generally won the day not because its arguments were always the most logical or cohesive. They won because they valued the real person over the legal principle. They answered questions not solely from the point of view of the book but from the living reality of the person sitting next to them. Unlike Shammai, Hillel would not slap a person who asked an outrageous question. He would give him an answer that led him to study. In following and expanding upon Hillel's perspective, Jesus did the same thing. Numerous examples testify to his focus on the person over the procedure, the felt needs over the legal precedent.

Perhaps the most famous example is the story of the woman accused of adultery in the Gospel of John. (Even though this story is found only in John, most scholars believed it emerged around the time as those of the Synoptic Gospels and fits more thematically there.) The accusation of adultery is delivered by the "legal experts" and "Pharisees" in front of the accused woman to Jesus at the Temple. They ask him what should be done, though it feels more like a rhetorical question than a legal one. He and they know the punishment for adultery is stoning. Jesus's answer both affirms the law and offers compassion for the woman. In other words, Jesus is both Hillel and Shammai. He is Shammai in that he does not simply abandon the law. He does not say that the punishment of stoning does not apply and that we can reject that biblical verse. Rather, he highlights the woman's humanity and the humanity of those around her by asking for one who has never sinned to throw the first stone. Like Hillel, Jesus does not say anything goes. Rather, he puts into action Hillel's maxim "what is hateful to you do not do to another." His rejection of the punishment of stoning also resembles Hillel's approach to the death penalty. The law exists, but it was rarely if ever enforced. By baiting him with the adultery charge, the woman's accusers are trying to put him in a bind. Either enforce the law or lose your compassion. Jesus takes the Hillel approach of not abandoning the law but putting the person's humanity first. In other words, his answer to the Pharisees was not un-Jewish. It was rooted in the compassion and humanity of the Pharisee Hillel.

QUESTIONS

Hillel is most remembered in Jewish tradition for a series of questions he asks in the Talmud. "If I am not for myself," he asks, "who will be for me? If I am only for myself, what am I? And if not now, when?"[1] These questions evoke self-evaluation. They challenge us as individuals and as members of a community. They serve as an extraordinary teaching tool. We can organize our lives around these questions.

Using questions to teach and evoke is a trademark of rabbinic Judaism. Indeed, the entire Talmud is structured around questions. These questions range from law and ethics to custom and history. The rabbis understood what Einstein reportedly would observe nineteen hundred years later: "If I had an hour to solve a problem and my life depended on the solution," he wrote, "I would spend the first fifty-five minutes determining the proper question to ask, for once I know the proper question, I could solve the problem in less than five minutes."

Sometimes elementary school teachers will say there is no such thing as a dumb question. They may be right in principle, but in matters of faith, there are questions that simply elicit information and those that shape behavior. The latter kind is both more interesting and useful in shaping our lives. In an age when we can look up almost any question of information on Google and Wikipedia, we crave and look for the questions that really engage and challenge us. Jesus draws from the Jewish tradition of asking these types of questions. Yes, the biblical heroes and rabbis did ask many kinds of information questions: Is this kosher or not? What time should we say the morning and evening prayers? Yet, more often than not, those information questions are springboards to deeper ones. And those deeper ones resonate to this day.

Among the most celebrated is the question Jesus asks during a storm on a ship in the Sea of Galilee. Jesus is sleeping serenely amid several of the disciples. The disciples are terrified. Drowning and death seem imminent. Rembrandt famously captured it in a painting entitled *The Storm on the Sea of Galilee*. We can almost see them asking themselves, "How can Jesus be so calm when we are about to drown?" In the Gospel of Mark they ask Jesus, "Teacher, don't you care that we're drowning?" Jesus responds to this question with a question of his own. "Why are you frightened?" he asks. "Don't you have faith yet?" (Mark 4:38-40).

We can immediately identify with the disciples. They are in mortal danger. Any sane person would feel terrified. And Jesus's answer seems aloof. He is not acknowledging their fear; he simply questions their faith.

This scene brings to mind a similar debate and conversation between Moses and

For Judaism and for Jesus, faith is not believing in certain things. It is, rather, about believing in someone.

the Israelites in the Sinai wilderness. It is a few days after the Israelites' escape from Pharaoh. The Israelites had witnessed magnificent miracles: the ten Plagues, the splitting of the Red Sea, and the subsequent drowning of the Egyptians. God had performed great miracles, freeing them after four hundred years of slavery. The Israelites' awe and faith had been confirmed when they crossed the sea and sang the "Song of the Sea," praising God as the "source of salvation." Yet, just a few days later, they are complaining to Moses about the lack of food and water. They miss the predictability of Egypt. They charge Moses (and thereby God, whose instructions Moses had followed) with taking them out of Egypt just to have them die in the wilderness.

Like the disciples on the ship, the Israelites' complaints seem warranted. They are stuck in the wilderness. They are lacking food. They probably do feel out of sorts, having had a drastic change in lifestyle in just a few days. Their lives may well be threatened by the barrenness of the wilderness and their vulnerability to potential attacks. They complain to Moses and Aaron. Initially God hears their complaints and responds with manna from heaven. Yet, the complaints continue. They are thirsty. Moses then responds in much the same way Jesus later would. In Exodus 17:2 we see the exchange, "Therefore the people quarreled with Moses and said, 'Give us water to drink.' And Moses said to them, 'Why do you quarrel with me? Why do you test the Lord?'" (my translation from the Hebrew). Moses is effectively saying, "Why don't you have faith in the Lord? God led you out Egypt. God provided you with manna. Have you still no faith?"

Notice the striking similarity: both Moses and Jesus respond with exasperation to their followers' lack of faith. They use an open-ended question to express their frustration. They use it to show their indignation. Why do they respond in this way? Why do they seem to let anger and disappointment overtake them? Some say Moses and Jesus believed their followers failed a test of faith. They should have known God could provide enough food and water and that the storm would not swamp the boat. Moses and Jesus were testing their people's faith, and both groups failed.

Perhaps. But I would turn to the Jewish idea of covenant to propose a different answer. *Covenant* refers to a sacred relationship. The first covenant is between God and humanity through Noah. The rainbow is the sign of that covenant. Noah promises to observe seven core laws, and God promises never to destroy the world again with water. The second covenant is between God and the Jewish people. Abraham promises to follow God's laws, as symbolized through circumcision. God promises Abraham land and descendants. This relationship goes through its ups and downs. It is tested, but it is also eternal. It is based on trust. It is what allows the Jewish people to always have hope because they trust that God will ensure their survival. And even when the Jewish people seem wicked and wayward, God knows they will eventually repent and return. The covenant is the framework in which that relationship exists.

In both of our stories, the people seem to be doubting the covenant. They have lost trust in the relationship. They are questioning its viability. Both groups are saying to Jesus and Moses: "How could you? You seem to have so much power, but now you are going to let us die!" Put differently, they are expressing the underlying feelings, "We have lost faith in you. You no longer have our trust. We can't rely on you anymore." And both Jesus and Moses respond with exasperation. They feel they have proven themselves to the people. Jesus has performed miracles. Moses has led the Israelites across the Red Sea. What more could they have done to earn the people's trust? In other words, it is not a failed test that disappoints Jesus and Moses. It is the breakdown of a relationship.

Ultimately, of course, both see to their followers' survival. God provides food and drink to the people. Jesus silences the storm. Yet, we sense a fraying of the relationship. We sense a disappointment by both Jesus and Moses toward their respective groups. Is there a lesson in this fraying? Why do the Hebrew Bible and the Gospels include it? Does it teach us something about faith?

THE MEANING OF FAITH

For Judaism and for Jesus, faith is not believing in certain *things*. It is, rather, about believing in *someone*. It is about trusting in a relationship. The Hebrew word often used for "faith" captures this idea. It is *emunah*. While usually translated as "faith," it really means "faithfulness." We express that faithfulness through words (prayer) and deeds. When we see Jesus the Jew, we begin to put less importance on what precisely we believe and greater emphasis on how we live in relationship with God. That relationship exists even through doubts and despair.

To better under this concept of faith, consider a deep friendship. If you are married, consider your spouse. These relationships are not based on a contract. We do not keep score. We trust. We believe in each other. We persist even when we make mistakes. When I counsel couples preparing to get married, I tell them there will be times when each feels as though he or she is doing 90 percent of the work in the relationship. But this lopsidedness is not grounds for dissolution. It is part of a relationship based not on "what can you do for me?" but "how can we sustain our partnership through life's uncertainties?"

I began to see how this idea is rooted in my faith shortly before getting married. There is a traditional Jewish custom of wrapping our arms in leather bands—known in Hebrew as *tefillin*—every day during morning prayers. Most Jews do not engage in this ritual, and up until my wedding day, I had never done so. It is quite time-consuming and seemingly unnecessary. I have always thought the words themselves are what we need to say and what God wants to hear. We do not perform physical acts to accompany them. Yet, an elderly rabbi whom I deeply respect asked me to put on tefillin on my wedding day. He said it would be good luck and mean a lot to him. So I thought, *I'm getting married, and I need all the luck I can get, so it can't hurt to try it.*

During the wrapping of tefillin, we say words from the biblical book of Hosea. We say them as we wrap the tefillin around our finger like a wedding ring.

> I will betroth you to me forever;
>   I will betroth you in righteousness and justice,
>   love and compassion.
> I will betroth you in faithfulness,
>   and you will know the Lord.
> (Hosea 2:19-20; my translation from the Hebrew)

As I said this, I realized the connection between faith and marriage. Every time we pray, we renew our relationship with

God. Faith means commitment to that relationship. The most prominent twentieth-century theologian to describe this truth was Martin Buber. In his book *I and Thou*, he said all real life is meeting.[2] We can also say faith is meeting God through our words and deeds. When we stop speaking, when we stop doing the little things that sustain a relationship, it falls apart. In other words, marriages and other relationships often fall apart because of indifference. We begin to pull out. We begin to doubt. We lose trust. That's what frustrated Jesus and Moses. The people lost trust. They did not doubt the existence of God. God was clearly evident to both the Israelites and the apostles. They lost trust in the relationship.

RETURNING TO QUESTIONS

Asking the right questions can remind us of why a relationship matters. When I counsel couples going through marital troubles, I often ask them what brought them together initially. I ask them about their values as a couple. I ask them what they love about each other. I ask them about the life they hope to create together. These questions remind them of who they are and why their relationship matters.

The right questions can reignite our faith as well. As we will see in the next chapter, that's part of the purpose of prayer. Prayer raises questions not about God but about our relationship with God. Are we living by our faith and not just professing it? Are we doing what God asks of us? Hillel, Moses, and Jesus all understood the power of the right question. When we ask them of and to ourselves, so can we.

CHAPTER 8

THE SHEMA

Frequently I am asked to officiate at weddings between a Jew and a Christian. In about half of those weddings, a minister or priest will join me. Some of my closest friends in the ministry have come from these ceremonies. We always try to create a balance that is respectful of both traditions. A few years ago one couple asked us to include what we deemed the central prayers from each of our traditions. I included the Shema (although it is not a traditional part of a Jewish wedding), and the priest included the Lord's Prayer. Both not only are familiar to Jews and Christians but also capture core theological ideas in brief and elegant language. They serve as a bridge between diverse religious traditions.

Both also played a significant role in Jesus's ministry. He knew and highlighted the centrality of the Shema. And he drew from a wide range of Jewish religious and political themes in crafting the Lord's Prayer. Though it is not recited in synagogues, the Lord's Prayer is, essentially, a Jewish prayer because of the language it uses and the teachings it conveys.

After reading the following two chapters, you will see why, and you will feel a deeper connection to these two prayers Jesus cherished.

You will also see the way Jewish prayer works. Jewish prayer, like Christian prayer, includes petition and praise and confession. All in all, Jewish prayer (like Christian prayer) reminds the person praying what matters most. The Lord's Prayer, for example, reminds the person praying of the imperatives to pursue justice in this world. In Judaism—and for Jesus—prayer is not an activity cut off from the rest of religious life. It is a core part of it. Prayer infuses life. It shapes the decisions and choices we make and the values we hold dear.

There is no separation between earth and heaven, between the material and the spiritual. All is spiritual.

Many prayers shape Jewish imagination—or, to put it differently, many prayers order Jewish affections—but none so centrally as the Shema.

WHAT IS THE SHEMA?

As the dad of a seven-year-old girl, I am unfortunately aware of the influence of Justin Bieber. I've had to answer several questions I'd have preferred not to and listen to music in the car I would have liked to silence. Yet, I was excited to share with my daughter Hannah one interesting fact I learned about Justin Bieber. According to his manager, who grew up regularly attending a conservative synagogue, Bieber says the opening line of the Shema prayer before every performance.[1]

The influence of the Shema clearly extends beyond its Jewish origins.

Two thousand years ago, Jesus was asked the most important commandment; he quoted the Shema: "You must love the Lord your God with all your heart, with all your being, and with all your mind" (Matthew 22:36-38). This line comes from the second part of the Shema, which is a three-part prayer taken primarily from chapter 6 of the Book of Deuteronomy. Its name derives from the opening verse: *Shema yisrael adonai eloyanu adonei echad*, "Hear, O Israel, the Lord is our God, the Lord is One." During worship, this verse was typically chanted by the prayer leader. It is followed by the congregational response, "Blessed is God's glorious kingdom forever and ever." This verse was added when the Shema become part of the regular worship service. The original text of the Shema then proceeds with "You shall love the Lord your God with all your heart, with all your being, and with all your strength" (6:5).

Jews often see the Shema as the essential description of Judaism because it contains the most coherent statement of monotheism: "The Lord is our God, the Lord is one." The story of Judaism's embrace of monotheism is a complex one, but according to Jewish tradition, Abraham lived in a world where multiple gods were worshiped. His great insight was seeing that one God created and will redeem the world, and that *God is both above and within us.* The Reform Jewish prayer book my synagogue uses contains a poetic evocation of this idea, describing God as being "as close to us as breathing, yet further than the most distant star."

This view of God shaped the world of first-century Jews. Yet, perhaps even more significant than the description of God as one is the meaning of the first word of the prayer, Shema. Shema means much more than listen or hear. Its full range of meaning cannot, in fact, be conveyed by any one word at all. Hebrew began as an oral language, and words had multiple meanings depending on the context in which they were used. Shema can mean to hear, to internalize, to answer, to act in accord with. The seventeenth-century King James Bible used a great word to translate Shema—to hearken! To hearken unto something is to respond to it. When God says *Shema Yisrael*, hear O Israel, it is an invitation for us to listen, to respond, to appreciate, to understand, to act. Our faith is a response to the oneness of God. We ground our lives in a relationship with the transcendent power of the universe. In other words, the Shema is about honoring the relationship between God and God's people. It is about acting in a way consistent with that relationship. Just as a marriage establishes boundaries in our personal relationship, so our relationship with God establishes boundaries and guidelines for our lives. The Shema is our call to recognize that relationship and live by its boundaries. It is a Jewish pledge of allegiance to God. We can see, then, why Jesus would identify it as among the most important commandments. It establishes the authority for all the other commandments. They all flow from it. The Ten Commandments, for example, would have no relevance if we did not believe in the Commander. The Shema affirms our belief in that Being.

In addition to establishing a relationship, the Shema also establishes a way of seeing the world. As we saw earlier, Albert Einstein once wrote that we can see either nothing as a miracle or everything as a miracle. It is possible, as many atheists have tried to prove, to see a world without God. The Shema, in contrast, teaches that the world is filled with God. In fact, the

Jewish mystics said *saying God is one is equivalent to saying the world is God*. There is no separation between earth and heaven, between the material and the spiritual. All is spiritual. The world is filled with God's presence. The Shema is our call to recognize that presence. It is no accident that the Shema is found in the Book of Deuteronomy. As we noted earlier, Jesus cites Deuteronomy more than any of the other books of Moses. And it is the books like Isaiah, rooted in the same worldview as that of Deuteronomy, that speak most frequently of *Kavod* Adonai, the presence, the indwelling of God in the world.

THE SHEMA OPENS UP A NEW WORLDVIEW: EVERYTHING IS GOD

One of the key biblical texts for the mystics—and likely for Jesus, as he cites it in Mark 12—was the story of Moses at the burning bush. Moses is tending sheep in the wilderness of Midian when he comes upon a bush that burns but is not consumed. Struck by this incongruence, he approaches the bush, and God speaks to him from it. The mystics interpreted this story in a unique way. They said the bush was always burning. It had never stopped. Many people had simply walked by it. Moses, however, stopped. He paused. He went and listened to it. The voice of God was always there. It did not speak especially to Moses. Rather, Moses was the first person to stop, notice, and listen to it. He heard God's voice, and then afterward the world never looked the same. Moses taught the world a new way of seeing the world. God was one: God's presence filled every place, every moment, every being.

Hearing the voice of God from the burning bush upended Moses's worldview. The ultimate aim of prayer is to do the same for us. When we say the Shema, we are meant to hear and see things differently. We are not meant to be like the Pharaoh of Egypt, who heard God's voice but did nothing in response to it. Rather, we are to be like Moses, who heard God's voice and changed his life. We do not even need such dramatic changes. We may simply need to pay more attention to what is around us.

Sometimes religious life can become too much of a routine. Prayer and ritual become rote. We say the words without feeling them. We perform the tasks without thinking about them. That requires less of us. It makes prayer a burden rather than an opportunity, a task rather than a vocation. I think Jesus cites the Shema to remind us what prayer means and asks us to do. Every word of the prayer is important. Here's why.

SHEMA, HEAR!

In Judaism, hearing is the most critical and perceptive of all the senses. It is through hearing that we attain truth. As Rabbi Norman Lamm put it, "Sound stands nearest to the purely spiritual among the phenomena of the world of the senses. Therefore, God has chosen it to be the medium of sensory revelation."[2] The Bible reinforces this idea frequently. At Mount Sinai the Israelites *heard* God's voice but did not see God.

While we live in a highly visual culture—think of the pervasiveness of television and screens—we can appreciate the power of hearing by thinking of the way a meaningful work of music affects us. I would bet you can think of some piece of music—perhaps a section of Beethoven's Ninth Symphony, or a religious chant, or the splash of ocean waves—that triggers your mind and heart in ways a screen or vision cannot. In the Bible, God's primary medium of communication is words. We hear God, we listen to God, and therefore we understand God's message. Indeed, as we noted, the word *Shema* does not simply refer to the auditory sense of hearing. It is so much more. Hebrew does not need a phrase like "active listening" because all the active parts of listening and responding are implied in the word *Shema*.

Like the ancient rabbi, Jesus understood this deeper meaning of the word *Shema*. To listen—and to listen for all that is truly being said—requires more from the heart than from the ears. Jesus cites this teaching—and it remains so central in Judaism today—because it upends our traditional way of experiencing the world. We typically say "seeing is believing." But in Judaism hearing is believing. And hearing demands a great deal from us. To listen with the heart takes time, energy, and empathy. It demands our full being. How often do we talk to a friend and then listen only for what we want to hear? How many times are we seeming to listen to someone and thinking about something else? How many of us have talked on the phone and read e-mail at the same time? To listen attentively is to be truly present, and it can be a struggle. Jesus also cites it because to listen is to model ourselves on God. God listens to our prayers. So we need to listen to them as well and listen to the prayers of others.

The intensely spiritual Russian writer Anton Chekhov describes the enormous challenge and sacredness of living this truth in his story "Misery." It is about a cab driver and his horse. They are parked on a street on a snowy winter night.

Finally they pick up a passenger. Soon after they begin the ride, the driver turns to the passenger and says, "Sir, my son died this week." "And what did he die of?" asks the passenger. The driver begins to tell him, but soon the passenger gets bored and says, "Just get a move on it, will you!" Soon the driver picks up a new passenger. He begins to tell him his son died, when this passenger says, "So what? We all must die. Get a move on it, old man, or we'll be late." Soon the driver returns to the stable. He ties up his horse and then sits down on a bench next to another driver. They begin talking. Soon he tells the other driver that his son died this week. Then, as he looks over, he sees the other driver has fallen asleep. He sighs then walks over to his horse and says, "You know, my son died this week . . ."[3]

People saw the driver. They may have even heard his words. But they did not listen. Jewish tradition asks us to say the Shema three times a day. Three times every day we need to remind ourselves to listen. And quite often we close our eyes when saying the Shema. Listening is not easy. It takes our full concentration. But when we listen—and listen truly—we witness God's image inside of us. We act as witnesses to God's presence. The Jewish sages illustrated this truth by pointing out an odd feature of the Torah scroll. All the letters in a Torah scroll are written in a prescribed manner. They have a standard size and shape. Yet, in the verse containing the Shema, two letters are enlarged. They are the last letter of the word *Shema*, which is a Hebrew *ayin*, and the last letter of the Hebrew word *echad* (one), which is a *dalet*. Together those two letters spell the Hebrew *ed*, which means "witness." To listen, to *shema*, is to witness God's presence on earth. The enlarged Hebrew letters are a clue to the reason Jesus cites it. He is instructing his disciples to be God's witnesses.

YISRAEL (ISRAEL)

Have you ever been in a big group of people, heard hundreds of voices singing the prayers, and felt a deep sense of connection to God? Some megachurches have this every week, but at my synagogue, we have to wait until the Jewish high holy days to gather more than a thousand. But when we do, something extraordinary happens. The chorus of voices seems to lift us up closer to God. Our prayers resonate more loudly when we say them together. We can pray alone. We can say the Shema alone. Indeed, we are supposed to recite it every night before bed. Yet, Jewish tradition teaches that God seeks the prayer of a community. A prayer quorum in Judaism—known as a *minyan*—requires ten adults. If ten people are not present, certain prayers are not said. This custom recognizes that the power of faith is not simply found in the words we say to God. It is found in the community we build with one another.

In the Shema, the word *Yisrael* refers to both the individual pray-er and the community. Israel is the proper name of one individual, the biblical patriarch also known as Jacob. In Genesis 16, after Jacob wrestles with the unidentified angel by the banks of the Jabbok River, God gives him an additional name: *Yisrael*. Among its several possible meanings is "one who struggles with God." The two names, Jacob and Israel, are used interchangeably throughout the rest of his life. The name Israel also comes to refer to his children and descendants as well. Communally, they become known as the people Israel.

Thus, we can read the Shema saying, "Hear, O Descendants of Israel." This interpretation opens it up to Christians who understand themselves as spiritual descendants of Jacob as well.

THE LORD IS OUR GOD. THE LORD IS ONE.

This phrase is Judaism's most concise statement of monotheism. Yet, monotheism is about much more than rejecting multiple gods. It is about the unity of heaven and earth. When we look at this phrase, we see that it conveys the multiple ways we experience God. To see this, we need to look at the Hebrew words. The English translation misses an important distinction in the Hebrew. Two different names are used for God. The first—which is translated as Lord—is the Hebrew YHVH, an unpronounceable set of Hebrew letters. Some have tried to pronounce it as *Jehovah* or *Yahweh*. The pronunciation is uncertain, however, because the Torah text includes no vowels, and the four Hebrew letters could be pronounced in multiple ways. The rabbis understand YHVH as God's proper name. It is the equivalent of our names, and we use YHVH when we pray and relate to God as a person. Since the name is unpronounceable, we substitute the word *adonai*, which means "Lord." Thus, in the Shema, when we see "Lord," we know it is a translation of the Hebrew proper name for God.

The other Hebrew word for God used in the Shema is *Elohim*. It is translated as "God." *Elohim* is the more abstract name of God. It is the way we refer to God in the third person. It is the equivalent of referring to "the doctor" rather than the doctor's first name. It is less intimate. It suggests a greater distance between God and humanity than the proper name YHVH.

Why do we need these two names for God? Because we relate to God in different ways. Sometimes, perhaps at the birth of a child, we are in awe of God's creation. We sense a magnificent power that makes life possible. That is the God of *Elohim*, of transcendence, of majesty. At other times, perhaps when a loved one dies, we turn to God in tears. We speak to God with sadness, seeking comfort and love. That is the God of YHVH, of relationship, of intimacy. These different names do not suggest different gods. They simply reflect different human experiences of the one God.

Another Jewish commentator—known as Rashi—offers a different explanation for the two names. The more abstract name, *Elohim*, evokes the present world where only some people believe in one God. YHVH evokes the world-to-come—after the Messiah has arrived and the dead have been resurrected—in which the entire world will know the God of Israel. The precise meaning of "know the God of Israel" is uncertain. Some sages see it as a time of universal conversion, where all people will essentially become Jewish. Other sages follow the teaching in the biblical Book of Micah, in which the prophet envisions a world in which all people will "do justice, embrace faithful love, and walk humbly with your God" (Micah 6:8). In other words, *all people will experience the one God of the universe through the idiom of their own religious community*. The only universal requirement will be acceptance of the Noahide laws, which include prohibitions on murder and stealing, the establishment of courts of justice, and acknowledgment of God. (These were the laws given to Noah when he began to rebuild humanity after the great flood.) Thus, according to Rashi, when we say the Shema, we are affirming acceptance of the one God by Israel and envisioning the eventual knowledge of God's power by the entire world.

WHY PRAYER MATTERS

Perhaps we need to take a step back and ask why we need all these interpretations. Aren't we simply supposed to say the prayers? Do we need to obsess so much about how we might interpret every syllable? Prayer is more than recitation of words. Judaism has a profound idea called *kavannah*. Kavannah is the intention, the mind-set, with which we come to pray. When we pray with kavannah, we focus our attention and intellect on the words we are saying. While there is wide latitude for defining the right mind-set with which we should pray, coming to prayer with a certain intention can elevate our spirituality. In other words, our mind-set affects the way we experience and hear God. If we say the words of the Shema filled with doubt and confusion, we will experience the words differently. Judaism has a place for doubt and discussion, of course. Yet, that place is not the sanctuary. The time is not during worship. Prayers cannot lift us up if we do not open our hearts and minds. Understanding the words can help them speak more directly to us. It can affect the tone and emotion with which we say them. An eighteenth-century rabbi, known as Baal Shem Tov (Master of the Good Name), taught that a person is where his or her mind is. In prayer, if our minds are on the God before whom we pray, we are truly communing with God.

We experience the God we commune with differently. Judaism and Christianity both believe in one God. Yet, Christianity has the notion of the Trinity. And in Judaism we have multiple names for God, and one of the most prominent names, *Elohim,* is actually a plural noun in Hebrew. We recognize that the names of God reflect our human experience of the Divine and not the nature of the Divine itself. Yet, what do we mean when we say God is one? Is our God one among many? What is the practical difference between praying to one God or two gods, or one God and no God? Monotheism is more complex than a simple number.

The answer is found in the Shema. The word *echad* means "one." It also means "singular," "alone," and even the noun "everything." God fills the universe. Every moment and every place is pregnant with God's presence. The Jewish mystics envisioned sparks of God inhering in everything. When we meditate on this idea during prayer, we begin to think and live differently. The great philosopher Spinoza encouraged his readers to view life from "the perspective of eternity."[4] When saying the Shema and concentrating on God's unity, we seek to fulfill this maxim and look at our lives from a larger canvas than we normally do. One of the twentieth century's most celebrated Jewish mystics, Rabbi Avraham Kook, pointed out that the first letter of the last syllable of the Shema is *chet*. In Hebrew all letters also have numeric values. *Chet* symbolizes the number eight. Rabbi Kook said the number eight is a symbol of eternity because it represents seven days of the week— the human cycle of time—plus one, which represents all that is beyond our time. To say God is one is to say God encompasses eternity. This teaching challenges us to consider what matters most in life.[5] When we look at our lives from the perspective of eternity, we might reconsider how we spend our time and how we treat those we love most.

To say God is one also suggests we are one. We are an integrated singular human being. This may sound like common sense, but it is an idea we often forget. When I was a child, I would occasionally misbehave. This happened most often when my parents were gone and I was with a babysitter. My mom would return, and the sitter would tell her what I did. She would then say, "Ah, I see Peter was acting up again. Peter ate the cinnamon rolls. Peter threw the Frisbee in the house. Why do you have to act like that, Peter? Why can't you be Evan all day?"

Somehow, according to my mom, Evan never did anything naughty. That was the doing of Peter. Now, I recognized that Peter was me. Yet, my mom was not doing good Jewish theology. We cannot offload the less positive parts of ourselves onto someone else. In theology, this practice is known as dualism, and it has presented difficulties for both Judaism and Christianity. Gnosticism—with which early Christianity and rabbinic Judaism struggled mightily—posited two dueling powers in the universe. They fought constantly with one another. Remnants of Gnosticism remain in Christianity with the idea of Satan, yet Satan is ultimately subordinate to God, making Christianity monotheistic. There is only one supernatural power in the universe. Prayer reconciles us to that one divine power.

This unity within God implies unity among we human beings, who are made in the image of God. When it comes to God's unity, the best Hebrew word is *shalom*. Shalom comes from the Hebrew root *sh-l-m*, which is translated as "peace." It means much more than peace as the absence of conflict. It implies peace as wholeness, completion, and harmony. It recognizes that peace is both an internal and external integration of different parts of ourselves. It is peace as convergence rather than divergence. A beautiful biblical description of this idea for Christians is found in Romans 5:1, where Paul says we have peace with God through Jesus. In other words, Jesus fulfills the meaning of the Shema for Christians. For Jews, the Shema highlights the unity of God in prayer so that we can develop it in life.

TIKKUN OLAM, REPAIR OF THE WORLD

The Shema proclaims God's unity, yet we see so much fragmentation and discord around us. Are we simply missing some underlying unity? Is it hidden from human eyes? Perhaps. The biblical Book of Job seems to make this argument. So do the Jewish mystics. Yet, first-century rabbis, including Jesus, and their successors perceived God's unity as a fact in heaven but an aspiration here on earth. In other words, they perceived a discord between the world as it is and the world as it ought to be. The Hebrew phrase *tikkun olam* means "repairing the world." It rests on the idea that the world is fragmented. Our actions can piece it together. As we restore the world to wholeness, we will perceive the unity and oneness of God.

This idea is based on a Jewish mystical story written after Jesus's life but which may have been orally transmitted during his lifetime. According to this story, the world was originally filled with God's presence. God was everywhere and everything.

In order to make room for human beings, however, God had to withdraw part of God's self from the universe. This voluntary withdrawal—known in Hebrew as *tzimtzum*—succeeded. In the process, however, sparks of God spread throughout the world. Some are hidden. Others are visible. Every time we pray and act according to God's will, we gather a spark into God. The more sparks we gather, the closer the world returns to the original perfection symbolized by the garden of Eden. When we say the Shema, we envision that state of perfection. We remind ourselves what God desires from us. And perhaps more subtly, we begin to see our own lives from God's perspective. Repairing the world becomes a more urgent imperative. We begin to move past our egocentric concerns and begin to pursue God's.

LOVE

*You shall love the Lord Your God, with All Your Heart,
with all your soul, and with all your strength.*

An old and unhealthy strand of Christian theology once saw Judaism as the religion of law and Christianity as the religion of love. Rooted in the writings of Augustine, these Christian readers contrasted what they saw as the legalistic passages of the Old Testament with what they took to be the more spiritually uplifting texts of the New. Many books and articles have been written refuting this point of view, and suffice it to say, love and law are central to both texts. Among the most eloquent calls to love is one found in the second verse of the Shema. It is the passage with which Jesus begins his answer to the question about the great commandment. "Love the Lord your God with all your heart, with all your soul, and with all your might." As we noted earlier, love is primarily an action in Judaism more than a feeling. The Jewish sages interpreted the phrase "Love the Lord your God with all your heart, with all your soul, and with all your might" as saying, among other possibilities, that we express our love of God with study, prayer, and action. But that is not all. The Torah deliberately focuses on each of these three parts of ourselves in order to illustrate what a loving God means for us.

With All Your Heart

The heart in Judaism is not just the seat of emotion. It is also, according to the rabbis, the source of the intellect. It shapes our attitude and our morality. To have a good heart is to live a morally upright and conscientious life. What, then, does it mean to love God with "all your heart"? We find a clue to the answer in an unusual feature of the Hebrew word for heart. That word is *lev*. *Lev* is typically spelled with a *lamed* and a *vet*. In the Torah—and in this instance only—the word *lev* has an additional *vet*. It is misspelled. Yet, according to the rules of rabbinic interpretation, God could never misspell a word. Therefore, there must be a reason for the extra letter. The reason, Maimonides suggests, is that the Torah is teaching us to love God both when we feel fortunate *and* when we are in despair. We need to love God during the good and the bad.

It's so much easier when things are good. If we are healthy and prospering, we can praise God without thinking too much about it. But when our lives take difficult and unexpected twists—when they become *undone*, in the phrase of my friend and writer Michele Cushatt—we also need to express that love.[6] When hope seems to fade—when frustrations mount and we do not know what to do—we need to find a way to express that love. This particular interpretation took on great meaning for many Jews after the Holocaust. How could we find the strength to love God when millions of fellow Jews were murdered? The answer many gave was another question. Seeing how much horror human beings can inflict on one another, how can one not turn to and love God? It is in the most difficult times that the love of God can help us realize we are more than biological animals. We are human beings created in God's image.

Loving through loss and despair is harder than it sounds. Pain can frequently lead to anger. I've seen this in marriages where a couple goes through a difficult experience together. Perhaps they have extraordinary difficulty with a child. Or perhaps one or both lose their jobs and financial collapse ensues. The pain can weaken and even destroy their relationship. Anger and frustration take up the emotional space love once held. The opposite, however, can also happen. The partners can learn about and love each other even more, deepening the relationship. They emerge stronger after one of them suffers an illness or a tragedy. Either scenario is possible. The Bible is urging us to love.

With All Our Soul

Martin Luther King Jr. once said, "If a man has not discovered something that he will die for, he isn't fit to live."[7] For King—and for religious leaders throughout history—their convictions were so strong as to lead them to die rather than abandon them. One of those leaders was a rabbi named Akiba. We discussed him in chapter 5. He lived in the first and second centuries of the Common Era and may have known the apostle Paul. Akiba was renowned for his love of God. He believed the Bible's most sacred book was the Song of Songs because it symbolized the love between God and the people of Israel. He saw the fulfilling of God's law and the studying of God's words as expressions of our love for God.

Akiba gave the most well-known interpretation of "with all our soul." He taught it as he awaited his execution as a martyr. He became a martyr for refusing to follow a Roman edict and give up teaching Torah. The Talmud reports he was arrested immediately after reciting and teaching the Shema in a public assembly. It describes his execution in excruciating detail. As he was tortured, he kept reciting the Shema. The executioner urged him to stop. Even his supporters—fellow rabbis in the crowd—urged him to stop. They said to him, "Do you need to suffer so much for the sake of Torah?" Akiba then answered with the following teaching:

> All my life I have wondered the meaning of the verse "You shall love the Lord your God with all your soul." I have loved God with all my heart. I have loved God with all my possessions [my might]. But I have never known what it meant to love God with all my soul. Now that I have come to this point—where God is about to take my soul—I know what it means.

Akiba then recited the Shema again and, according to the Talmud, his soul departed him, and he died as he said the word *echad*.[8]

This powerful story does not mean we have to be martyrs in order to love God with all our souls. Rather, we love God with all our souls when we are ready to die for the sake of God's truth. It is the psychological readiness to die for what we believe that constitutes love with all our souls. It need not involve the act of martyrdom itself.

If this idea seems far-fetched and more consistent with an age of religious fundamentalism, consider some of the heroes of our world. Think of Nelson Mandela, who clearly was willing to die and suffered twenty-seven years of prison to achieve freedom in his homeland. Or consider persecuted religious minorities—Christians in the Middle East, Buddhists in Tibet, Jews throughout history—who have risked death to practice their faith. Every year on the Jewish holiday of Yom Kippur we recite a prayer called the *Kol Nidre*. The phrase means "All our vows," and it asks God to forgive us for the promises we sincerely make but cannot keep. The prayer was originally said by Jews who were forced to convert to Catholicism by the Inquisition in fourteenth-century Spain but continued to practice their Judaism in secret. They would gather every year on *Kol Nidre* and sing the prayer. Had they been caught, they would have been murdered. On the holiest day of year—Yom Kippur—we recount that willingness to die.

This exercise can teach us even if we struggle with faith and beliefs. Though it may sound gruesome, imagining our own death can help us learn how to live. We see that our years are limited. We see how valuable every moment is. One of the Jewish customs on *Kol Nidre* is wearing a white garment known as a *kittel*. Men are supposed to wear a kittel at their weddings, on every *Kol Nidre*, and as a burial shroud. *Life becomes more sacred when we recognize its limits.* Steve Jobs, the founder of Apple, put this truth in dra-

The way we live influences the way others live. If we show a deep love of God, we spread it into the lives of others.

matic terms in a commencement address he gave at Stanford University in 2005. "Remembering that I'll be dead soon," he said, "is the most important tool I've ever encountered to help me make the big choices in life. Because almost everything—all external expectations, all pride, all fear of embarrassment or failure—these things just fall away in the face of death, leaving only what is truly important."[9] To love God with all our souls is to love the limited time on earth God gave us.

With All Our Strength

This last phrase in the commandment to love God seems out of place. The reason is that three-part progressions in the Torah typically end with the hardest one. What can be harder than giving one's life to God? The rabbis consistently interpreted "with all your strength" as meaning with your financial resources. Is giving money really harder than being willing to die for the sake of God? In other words, do some people consider money more important than life itself?

Indeed. The Talmud tells an intriguing story about a man who crosses a field filled with thorny plants. He pulls up his pants to avoid getting them ripped. Meanwhile, he lets his legs get bloody and cut up. At least, he reasons, his pants were saved. If this scenario seems a little extreme, consider the lengths some people go to save a dollar. I'm not talking about people who are struggling financially. I'm talking about people who get a dangerous cut or break a bone and refuse to go to a doctor because it might cost $100. Or people who will endure a painful walk in the ice cold to avoid a $10 cab ride. Sometimes such stories are funny and reflect a frugal mind-set. Other times they simply reflect the extraordinary and irrational risks people will take to save a small amount of money. As one rabbi once noted in writing about this verse of the Shema, "In Nevada, where gambling is legal and every hotel has a casino, hotel room windows are specially designed not to open more than a crack—so people who lose money gambling won't be tempted to jump out the window. Yes, for some, money is more important than life itself."[10]

Still, even if we can argue that the value of money trumps the value of life for some people, what does it mean to love God with all our resources, with all our financial means? To what lengths are we supposed to go to illustrate our love of God? We need to recognize that, taken to an extreme, this teaching can be quite dangerous. Think about televangelists who prey on down-and-out people and beg them to donate their last dollars as a sign of faith.

The rabbis addressed this issue in a creative way. They suggested loving God with all our resources did not necessarily mean giving all of our resources over to God. The obligation to give charity is addressed elsewhere in Jewish law. Loving God with all our might implied an attitude toward life rather than a specific monetary obligation. One rabbi illustrated this idea with an intriguing and humorous example. He taught that a person's love of God should be so great that it flows into their very possessions so that they, too, glow with a love of God. He cites the example of a donkey of one of the great rabbis in the Talmud. This donkey refused to eat nonkosher food! The rabbi's love and commitment to God were so strong that they flowed into his donkey. This bit of rabbinic hyperbole teaches a deeper lesson. Our love of God can teach and inspire others. The way we live influences the way others live. If we show a deep love of God, we spread it into the lives of others.

CONCLUSION: WHAT THE SHEMA CAN MEAN

The Shema is the core prayer of Judaism. Jesus undoubtedly said it throughout his life. Yet, it is not well-known among many Christians. Aside from its connection to Jesus, is there a way it can become more meaningful? One potential approach is to think about the three kinds of love of God as corresponding to the three manifestations of God as understood in the Christian trinity. The Father may feel the love of our might, the Son may feel the love of our hearts, and the Holy Spirit may feel the love of our souls. Part of the beauty of the Trinity is that it acknowledges that God is one while allowing believers to relate and pray to God in multiple ways. In other words, the Trinity reflects an early Jewish idea that the Torah has multiple entry points. It's the same Torah, but sometimes we see varied manifestations of it at different points in our lives. We also love God in multiple ways. Sometimes that love takes the form of prayer. Other times it is expressed in study and actions. Love is not only a noun but also a powerful verb. And the Shema leads us to it.

I witnessed this lesson most powerfully at a recent Bat Mitzvah ceremony at my synagogue. In Judaism a young woman becomes a Bat Mitzvah when she blesses and reads from the Torah scroll at age twelve or thirteen. She is then considered a young adult in the Jewish community and follows more of the commandments such as fasting on the Day of Atonement and praying regularly. Becoming a Bat Mitzvah is marked by a special ceremony at the synagogue on the Sabbath. The Bat Mitzvah leads the worship, teaches about the prayers, reads from the Torah, and delivers the sermon.

A recent Bat Mitzvah focused much of her teaching and preaching on the Shema. It happened to be the section of the Torah she read. Her remarks not only left many in tears but also reflected her personality. They inspired her friends and guests. They showed the way prayers lift up our hands and hearts. Here's what she said:

> The Shema teaches us to love God with all of our essence: our heart, soul, and strength. You don't have to be standing up here like I am, translating and interpreting prayers, to love God. If you see someone sitting alone at lunch, invite them over to your table. If you see that someone at dance class isn't understanding the newest combination, help them out. If you think someone's having a bad day, make them feel better. Believe it or not, all of these things are expressions of our love for God.

To that we can only say *amen*.

CHAPTER 9

THE LORD'S PRAYER

When I have spoken at churches and asked how many people know the Shema, few hands are raised. When I ask about the Lord's Prayer, however, every hand shoots up. When I officiate at interfaith weddings where it is recited, almost every face on the Christian side of the gathering can be seen mouthing it. Sometimes those on the Jewish side may be saying it as well, since many public schools required its recitation prior to 1962.[1]

The prayer is found in the Gospels of Matthew and Luke, though the Matthew (chapter 6) version is the more familiar. Scholars do not know which version is closer to what Jesus taught, but both fit very well within the context of first-century Jewish life. Indeed, they do more than simply reflect first-century Jewish life; they offer a radical response and approach to it. They suggest that Jesus was a "rebel rabbi," drawing new truths from ancient Jewish traditions. As scholar Amy-Jill Levine has pointed out, "When placed in a first-century Jewish context, the prayer recovers numerous connotations that make it both more profound and more political. It fosters belief, promotes justice, consoles with future hope, and recognizes that the world is not always how we would want it."[2] Levine's research on the prayer has profoundly influenced my own reading and shapes what follows.

Since it is such a well-known and frequently recited prayer, learning the Lord's Prayer in a new way can bring us into a more intimate relationship with God. We can imbue familiar words with new meanings. I saw this happen at a recent church where I spoke. The congregation had gathered after worship in the fellowship hall to hear me speak. Unbeknownst to me, the minister had a plan. After he introduced me, he asked the group to rise and recite the Lord's Prayer. Everyone sat down and I prepared to speak about my announced topic: What Every Christian Needs to Know about Passover (the subject of my previous book). Then, before I could get a word out, a man in the front row asked me about the Lord's Prayer. "I've heard it's a Jewish prayer," he said. "Is that right?" I started to talk about it, and then more questions arose, and by the end of my allotted forty-five minutes, Passover had been forgotten and we had spoken only of the Lord's Prayer. They asked me if we could recite it again at the end so they could feel it in a new way. Perhaps the same can happen to you.

"OUR FATHER, WHO IS IN HEAVEN"

References to God as "our Father" do not appear in the Hebrew Bible. God does refer to the Israelites as His "first born," though we do not see the people use a familiar term referring to God. God is most often called by the proper name YHVH or *Elohim*. During the second Temple period of Jewish history—the years between about 530 BCE and 70 CE—references to God as father begin to appear. They all occur within the phrase "father in heaven." This phrase suggests the reason for this development. Heaven symbolizes a distant place. It is high above us. It suggests God's transcendence, God's awe and power. "Father," however, suggests intimacy and closeness. "Our Father" is someone we can relate to. Calling God "Our Father in heaven" bridges the distant and the intimate. It develops closeness while preserving God's majesty. It signifies trust in a higher power. One verse in the Talmud describes this connotation succinctly: "Upon whom can we rely? Our father who is in Heaven."

Some scholars have suggested that Jesus introduced the more intimate "our Father" reference to God as a way of inviting the disciples into a closer relationship with God. One scholar even suggested "our daddy" as the best translation for the Aramaic *abba*. This greater intimacy, he argued, put Jesus at odds with the Jewish leaders of the time, who were more interested in God as a distant lawgiver. This interpretation has little basis to support it. As Professor Levine has pointed out, one of the scholars who initially made this argument later retracted it and called it "naivety." The truth is Jesus was working within a Jewish context that sought to balance God's power with His love and the personal with the universal.

The use of the term *father* in rabbinic sources and by Jesus also introduces a new kind of love—filial love—into the relationship between God and the people. This is a critical development in religion. In addition to covenant, the other key metaphor for the relationship between God and the Israelites in the Bible is king and people. In this metaphor, the people ultimately serve the king. That's what a king's people did in the ancient Near East. The story of the Exodus is not simply the journey from slavery to freedom. It is the journey from slavery to Pharaoh to service to God. The people's responsibility to God is service, and God's responsibility to the people is protection.

The shift in metaphor from God as ruler to God as father changes the responsibilities of the relationship. The people still serve God, but they also love God, and they love in a way a child loves a parent. And more importantly, God also loves the people. A midrash likely composed around the time Jesus lived introduces this idea into Jewish literature. It is taken from the book of legends about Exodus known as the *Mekhilta*. Commenting on the verse from Exodus, "'And God goes before them during the day,' R. Yosse the Galilean taught: Were it not written in scripture one could not say it—like a father carrying a lantern before his son, and like a master carrying a lantern before his servant." In other words, God does the opposite of what a father or master typically does. Instead of having the servant carry the lamp to light the way on a walk, God the master carries the lamp to light the way for the servant. Instead of a son carrying the light for his father, God the Father carries the light for His son, to the people of Israel.[3] What is the justification for this deviation from normal social structures? Love. In the midrash, it is God's love that leads God to alter normal behavior and serve his children. Jesus draws from this new emphasis on the centrality of filial love in the opening line of the prayer.

In addition to love, "our Father" introduces a political dimension into the divine-human relationship as well. First-century Jews lived under the rule of the Roman Empire. The emperor (the Caesar) was often referred to as father. The Roman historian Dio makes this point, suggesting it helped humanize the relationship between the ruler and the ruled. Jesus and other first-century rabbis, however, make clear that our father is in heaven. In other words, the true father we serve is not Caesar.

Clarity about the limits of Caesar's power was not something Roman authorities would take kindly to. Thus, we have texts in both the New Testament ("give unto Caesar what is Caesar's and unto God what is God's") and the Talmud ("the law of the state is the law") that delineate the earthly ruler's power as well.[4] Pointing to God as our father, however, gives an equality to all people in the world. It renders meaningless any differences between Jews and gentiles, Roman citizens and conquered people. God is the father of each of them. Once again, Jesus is a rebel rabbi.

"Uphold the Holiness of Your Name"

This next line echoes one of Judaism's most sacred prayers, known as the *Kaddish*. That prayer opens with the words "Magnified and Hallowed Be Your Great Name." The Kaddish is now Judaism's primary prayer of mourning. In the first century, however, it was a prayer said in the house of study. When a teacher would finish delivering a lesson or lecture, the students would rise and recite the prayer. It honored God's wisdom as passed through the teacher. It may have become associated with mourning when it became customary to say the prayer upon the death of a great scholar or teacher. Its primary theme is God's strength and the establishment of God's rule on earth.

Both the Kaddish and the Lord's Prayer focus on the sanctity of God's name. God's name is a source of complex theological reflection in Judaism. Jewish mysticism holds that the people once knew how to pronounce God's proper name, which is indicated by the Hebrew letters *yud, hay, vav, hay*. The letters themselves can be pronounced multiple ways, as we learned in chapter 8. But, one needs to know the vowels to pronounce them correctly, and those values are absent from the Torah scroll. Every year on the holiest day of the year, Yom Kippur, it is said that the high priest would pronounce God's name in the holiest place in the Jerusalem temple. When the Temple was destroyed, however, and the high priest was no more, no one knew how to pronounce God's proper name. It remains a mystery. Jewish tradition says it will only be known in the world to come.

We are vessels for an immortal spirit.

In the Kaddish and the Lord's Prayer, God's name signifies both God's power and reputation. *When we ask to uphold the holiness of God's name, we are praying that people around the world recognize the wisdom and power of our God.* We are asking that the name of God influence people's behavior and beliefs around the world, echoing what God said to Abraham: "All the world will be blessed through you" (Genesis 22:18; my translation from the Hebrew). We are dreaming the same dream Isaiah did when he envisioned the nations of the world streaming into Jerusalem to learn the word of God. We are also calling upon ourselves to hallow God's name. Jewish tradition understands human beings as God's partners in the ongoing creation of the world. In Christian terms, our lives are the best evangelistic tool we have. We hallow God's name when we live by God's law. Thus, when we say, "Uphold the holiness of your name," we are also praying to live in a way that leads others to hallow God's name.

The Lord's Prayer also shares with the Kaddish a rhythmic power. Prayer shares many literary traits with poetry. They both seek to invoke, inspire, and speak to the heart as well as the mind. They have a rhythm and flow that carries the words and feelings along with them. And they both generate gut reactions within us. We feel a connection to the best poetry and prayer that is often inexplicable. Jews feel that connection with the Kaddish. At funerals when we recite it, I see worshipers closing their eyes and saying the words from memory. They may not even know what they mean, since the prayer is in Aramaic, but they gain comfort from its words. The same is true for the Lord's Prayer. Though my direct experience of its power is limited, pastors and priests I've talked to describe its unconscious influence on those who recite it.

"BRING IN YOUR KINGDOM"

The kingdom of God (or *kingdom of heaven*) is a frequent phrase in the New Testament. It refers to the messianic age. The time, as the Prophets envisioned, when "Nation will not take up sword against nation; / they will no longer learn how to make war" (Isaiah 2:4). It is a time when God's sovereignty will replace that of all earthly rulers. The rabbis did not refer to this period as a kingdom. Rather, they described it as the *olam ha-bah*, the world to come. The *olam ha-bah* is different from the immediate afterlife. It is a period that will come at some later point, though all who have lived will participate in it.

Many Christians and Jews believe the idea of an *olam ha-bah* originated in Christianity. They contrast a Jewish belief in this world with a Christian belief in the afterlife. In fact, however, Judaism had a rich tradition of insight and speculation on the afterlife from which Jesus drew. It developed primarily between 300 BCE and 200 CE, a time when Judaism was profoundly influenced by Greek ideas. In the Bible, the afterlife is simply a place called *sheol*, where souls gather. It is neither good nor bad. Influenced by the Greek understanding of form and matter—the matter deteriorates but the form is eternal—Jewish sages of the period developed the idea of a soul (*neshama*) that is eternal and returns to God when our matter (body) is no longer. In other words, the death of our bodies is not the death of our souls. They continue to live with God. Other Jewish thinkers built on this idea to argue for reincarnation in different bodies or some other kind of physical container for the soul. What is most important, however, is acknowledging that this world is not the end of our lives. That belief opens up the possibility for divine intervention that affects us even if we do not witness it as well as hope when the righteous seem to suffer in this world.

By the beginning of the second century of the Common Era, Judaism began to place less emphasis on the afterlife. This development may have resulted from the concomitant rise in emphasis Christian thinkers placed on it. In other words, Judaism defined some of its core beliefs in opposition to Christianity. Yet, I am grateful Christianity both preserved and elaborated on Jewish teachings about the afterlife. It left the door open for Jews to rediscover our faith's understanding of it, and I have seen many people comforted and inspired by the idea that we are more than physical beings. We are vessels for an immortal spirit.

"SO THAT YOUR WILL IS DONE ON EARTH AS IT'S DONE IN HEAVEN"

Another way of saying this verse would be "May what happens on heaven and earth reflect God's will." The critical word in this verse is *will*. The Hebrew word for it is *ratzon*, which can also mean desire. The tension arises from the question of who is responsible for ensuring God's will be done. Is it all up to God? Or do human beings play a role as well? Put differently, do we human beings have free will, and can we use that free will to implement God's will on earth? Or is choice an illusion, and God's will is served whether we choose to follow it or not?

These questions divided Jews during the first century. The priests generally believed everything was in the hands of God. The realization of God's will depended exclusively on God. The Pharisees, by contrast, believed in a partnership. As historian Josephus put it, "[The Pharisees] say that certain events are the work of Fate [that is, Providence], but not all; as to other events, it depends upon ourselves whether they shall take place or not, specifically in matters of righteous and wicked behavior."[5] In other words, our deeds matter. We decide whether we act in a righteous or wicked way, and these decisions shape whether the will of God is realized or not. The Pharisees (later the Rabbis) made decisions and sought to implement God's will by following the laws of the Torah. Thus, God's will is done on earth through obedience to Torah.

Most scholars believe Jesus followed the Torah closely his entire life. In doing so, he also, according to later verses in the Gospel of Matthew, embraced the rabbinic idea known as "building a fence around the Torah." This is the practice of taking precautionary steps to avoid the temptation to violate the laws of the Torah. It was a way of making extra-certain to follow God's will. The rabbis would make these precautionary steps part of the corpus of Jewish law in the Talmud. One example would be avoiding the mixing of milk and meat in one's dining in order to avoid the remote possibility of "boiling a kid in its mother's milk" (Deuteronomy 14:21; my translation from the Hebrew). We might be consuming cheese from a calf whose mother was the cow whose meat we are eating. As Professor Levine points out, Jesus builds a fence around the Torah in another section of the Sermon on the Mount: the so-called Antitheses (Matthew 5:21-47). They begin, "To those who heard it said, 'You shall not murder,' Jesus says, 'If you are angry with a brother or sister, you shall be liable to judgment.' To those who heard it said, 'You shall not commit adultery,' Jesus says, 'Everyone who looks at a woman with lust has already committed adultery with her in his heart.'"[6] Jesus notes the Torah law, and then makes it stricter.

These are well-known teachings of Jesus. What is less well-known, as we now see, is that they are rooted in the Jewish custom of building a fence around the Torah. If this practice strikes you as too odd or legalistic, consider ways you might "build a fence around the Torah" in your own life. If you are on a diet and at a restaurant, do you avoid looking at the dessert menu? Perhaps it might be too tempting, and you'd rather avoid tingling the temptation altogether? Or perhaps you need to arrive at a meeting on time. You know you have a propensity to be late. Perhaps you write the time of the meeting in your calendar for fifteen minutes before it starts. Then you are more likely to arrive by the time it really begins. To use contemporary terminology, building a fence around the Torah is another phrase for "life-hacking." We build tricks into our practices so that we are sure to keep our commitments. It is very serious life-hacking, however, because we are working with God's word. The hacks are a way we recognize our human fallibility and build in ways to make sure we follow God's word.

"GIVE US THIS DAY OUR DAILY BREAD"

We can divide Jewish prayer into three categories: praise, gratitude, and petition. Prayers of praise highlight God's attributes. Prayers of gratitude thank God for the blessings we enjoy. Prayers of petition ask God for things and qualities of character. Most Jewish prayer falls into the first two categories. And on the Sabbath, we refrain from petitionary prayer altogether. The Lord's Prayer is primarily praise and petition. Up until this verse, we have seen all praise. We now move to petition. (I use the King James translation for this verse because it more closely parallels its Hebrew Old Testament sources.)

The first object for petition is "our daily bread." Bread is a symbol here for food in general. It is also the symbol for spiritual sustenance. In these two roles, *Jesus's "daily bread" echoes the daily manna God provided the Israelites in the wilderness.* This manna assuaged the Israelites' hunger. It also answered their fear of being abandoned in the wilderness. The manna was a sign of God's presence. Jesus also echoes the manna with a subtle repetition. When I teach about this prayer, I always point out that Jesus says, "Give us *this day* our *daily* bread." These words are redundant. One of the cardinal Jewish rules of biblical interpretation is that every word matters. God does not put extra words in the Bible that have no unique meaning or purpose. Why, then, does the text not just say, "Give us our daily bread" or "Give us our bread today"? Why does it say "this day" and "daily" bread? I think the repetition is meant to remind us of the double portion of bread God gave Israelites on the Sabbath in the wilderness. On the sixth day of the week God would provide enough bread for the Israelites for two days. They did not gather on the Sabbath. This double portion reminds us once again of our dependence on God and God's generosity in sustaining us. Even when refraining from work, as on the Sabbath, God provides.

Another possible explanation for the repetition is that it reminds us of a miracle in the way God provided manna in the wilderness. Somehow, as the text points out in Exodus 16, God provided the right amount of food for each person individually. "The Israelites did so, some gathering more, some less. But when they measured it with an omer, those who gathered much had nothing left over, and those who gathered little had no shortage; they gathered as much as each of them needed" (Exodus 16:17-19; my translation from the Hebrew). Every day God provided precisely for every person's unique daily needs. We have no need for hoarding or worry. Gratitude is the prayer's lesson. Faith is what it engenders. What began in the Sinai wilderness finds its way into the Lord's Prayer.

One final possibility is that "daily" is repeated as a plea for the Messiah. In other words, it is a way of asking God to give us today the bread prepared for us in the world to come. It is a messianic cry. This interpretation reflects an ancient Jewish vision of the world to come (also known more popularly as "heaven") as a grand banquet. This vision is articulated in Isaiah 25:6, in which Isaiah envisions a grand banquet on a mountaintop. We also see it in the Talmud, in which the rabbis call this world a "vestibule for entry into the grand banquet hall," which is the world to come.[7]

This idea has carried over into contemporary Jewish life in how we celebrate the Sabbath. At my house—and many other places where I've had a Sabbath dinner—the food is overflowing. We eat more than we would at a regular dinner. In fact, one popular Jewish custom is skipping lunch on Friday to become extra appreciative of the Sabbath food. We also invite guests to share the meal. The Jewish mystics described the Sabbath meal as "a taste of heaven." Consider the implications of this idea. *We can taste the bread of the next life here in this life.* Christian worship incorporates some of this idea in the communion table, where food and wine are shared. One literally gets a taste of heaven at the Lord's table.

"FORGIVE US OUR DEBTS, AS WE FORGIVE OUR DEBTORS"

Some may find the transition between bread and debt rather jarring. (Again, I am using the King James version.) One is our daily nourishment. The other makes us think about banks. Yet, they are two sides of the same coin. First, both bring to mind economic justice. The poor strive to have enough food to eat and to not have outrageous debts hanging over them. While having enough food may seem the more urgent and important priority, debt can leave someone poor and despondent for a long time. A member of my synagogue recently started an organization focused on fighting debt's crippling power. She works with low-income workers to help them lobby their employers to include credit counseling as an employee benefit. This may seem strange at first. Shouldn't the top priority of employees be getting better salaries and working conditions? Why push for credit counseling? Because they recognize the lingering power of bad credit, which is caused by excessive debt. They can't buy a home. They can't buy a car. They have to pay exorbitant amounts of interest. Debts cripple.

In biblical times excessive debt also led to slavery. Initially, the Hebrew Bible allowed both Israelites and foreigners to pay off debt by working as indentured servants. We see this clearly in the books of Exodus and Deuteronomy. Yet, the rupture this debt created within the community became evident. By the time of the Book of Nehemiah, which describes the fifth-century BCE Jewish community in Palestine, tension mounted in the community between lenders and borrowers. Nehemiah urged the aristocrats to stop lending with interest to their fellow Israelites. They obliged, though other forms of debt still accrued. The tension between fostering the common good and accumulating wealth challenged biblical Jews. It continues to challenge all of us today. Like Nehemiah, Jesus was emphasizing the transformative power of forgiving debts within a community. Indeed, while debt and slavery characterized biblical society, the Hebrew Bible created systems for forgiving debts at appropriate times. That system was built around the Sabbath.

We noted earlier the Jewish concept of the Sabbath as a taste of the world to come. The Sabbath was not just a rest from the routine of daily life. The concept of the Sabbath extended to land and debts as well. The Hebrew word *shabbat* is derived from the Hebrew root *sh-v-yah*, which means "seven." The Sabbath is the seventh day of the week. The Sabbatical year is the seventh year of a seven-year cycle. And the year after seven seven-year cycles is called the Jubilee year. It is, effectively, the Sabbath of Sabbatical years. *Each of these Sabbaths has a forgiveness of debts associated with it.* The weekly Sabbath is a day when all labor was forbidden. This rest applied to animals and slaves, which were groups considered property of and therefore beholden to the landowner. The use of their labor was forbidden on the Sabbath day.

During the seventh year, all monetary debt was also to be forgiven. Scholars do not know whether the law was ever implemented, but conceptually it suggests God envisioned an Israelite society in which excessive debt did not become a burden. During the Jubilee year, the Sabbath of the Sabbatical years, all property was to be restored to its original owners. Again, scholars debate whether this law was ever implemented. Determining the original owners is fraught with problems, given that the land was conquered by Joshua and the twelve tribes. Yet, the principle illustrates God's concern with *restorative righteousness.* Forgiveness of debts helped restore people to their original state of freedom. Letting the land rest for a year helped restore its richness. Restoring people to their original landholdings helped ensure that social inequality did not become a permanent fixture of Israelite society.

In the context of this prayer, however, forgiveness is about much more than money. (That's why some versions of the prayer replace *debts* with *trespasses*.) It is about the society God envisions and calls upon us to realize. Forgiveness is an essential part of it. We will all have times to be forgiven and to forgive. To illustrate this truth, I often ask my confirmation class to imagine a world without forgiveness. Grudges would be held indefinitely. Cycles of violence would continue for generations. Even as we recognize its necessity, forgiveness can seem countercultural. People should pay for their crimes. Actions should have consequences. According to Jewish tradition, God recognized this tension and sought to create a world balanced between *tzedek* (justice, or rule of law) and *rachamim* (mercy, or forgiveness). The Lord's Prayer recognizes this tension and asks us to err on the side of mercy. The name we give to God's mercy is grace.

"AND LEAD US NOT INTO TEMPTATION, BUT DELIVER US FROM EVIL"

We noted that the temptations in the wilderness described in Matthew are truly tests of faith. Temptation and tests go together. This understanding informs the meaning of this particular verse of the Lord's Prayer. We are asking God to refrain from challenging us with similar tests of faith. We are asking God not to force us to choose to be martyrs. This was a real fear of Jews during the time of Jesus, as the Romans cracked down on expression of Jewish practices and teaching of Torah. Several rabbis were burned alive for refusing to denounce their faith, and we remember them every year on the Day of Atonement. While we praise those who withstood such tests of faith, we do not wish them for ourselves. The paradigmatic example of this is Abraham. Who would wish to be put to the test of sacrificing one's son out of loyalty to God? Who would want to lose everything and fall into utter misery, as did Job, in order to prove their faith? Abraham was likely tempted to simply abandon the God who had spoken to him. Job was tempted to abandon his faith and, as his friends suggested, curse God. The temptation for first-century Jews may well have been to submit to the Romans and inform on their fellow Jews. We ask God to have mercy on us and not subject us to such painful trials.

Another possibility advanced by some scholars is that the temptation is violence. According to this point of view, Jesus is committed to nonviolent resistance to the Roman Empire. Several Jewish groups during the time did embrace this approach, most notably the Pharisees, who were the only Jews to survive in larger numbers. Given the degree of Roman persecution, such groups were undoubtedly tempted toward violence. Perhaps Jesus is urging God to help Jews resist that temptation and deliver them from the evil such hatred represents.

Prayer does not instantly make us different people. Over time, it smooths out the rough edges. It moves us closer to the core of our being—to the image of God within us.

A more plausible interpretation of the second part of this verse, however, is that evil symbolizes the "evil one": Satan. Satan, as we have discussed, serves as an active participant in God's testing of the Jewish people. The prayer is therefore asking God not to test us and not to let Satan test us either. Professor Levine notes how this interpretation fits the typical features of first-century Jewish prayer. "To put this final pair of verses, 'Do not bring us to the test, but rescue us from evil,' on the colloquial level, the couplet may be seen as saying, 'Look, God, I don't need testing from you, and I certainly don't need being brought to the test by Satan.' Provocative, directly related to human experience, intimate enough with God to be direct, it is an ideal prayer for a first-century Jew."[8]

CAN WE TEST GOD?

When teaching about this prayer, I've frequently received a thoughtful and difficult question. According to the Bible, God tests us. We see it with Abraham, Job, Jesus in the wilderness, and several others. Yet, why is it unacceptable for us to test God? Indeed, in Deuteronomy 6:16, a verse Jesus cites in the wilderness, Moses condemns the people for daring to attempt to test God. Is this a double standard? Is the Bible encouraging blind obedience? Would we respect a parent who says to his or her child, "I am going to test your love for me all the time. Yet, you are never permitted to question my love for or commitment to you." Probably not.

The Jewish idea of covenant helps us make sense of this difficulty. God is the senior partner in the covenant, and God's commitment is steady and unyielding. The Hebrew Bible emphasizes this several times, noting that God will bring the Israelites on eagles' wings from the four corners of the earth when the exile is over. God's commitment to the people of Israel is unflappable. We are, of course, permitted to question decisions. Abraham wonders why God would decide to destroy the entire cities of Sodom and Gomorrah. Moses questions God's inclination to destroy the people after they construct a golden calf. But in each of these instances, if we read the texts carefully, we see that God is inviting our biblical heroes to question God's decision as a sign of commitment to the covenant. In other words, God is inviting the questions in order to help the Israelites learn and grow, much as a parent would invite thoughtful questions in teaching a child. *What seems like a test of God is a lesson for us.*

To see the way this works, consider the discussion between God and Abraham when God decides to destroy the towns of Sodom and Gomorrah. Before God reveals God's plans, we see an internal monologue from God, the only instance of this in the Hebrew Bible. God says, "Shall I hide from Abraham what I am about to do. . . . For I have chosen him so that he may instruct his children and his household after him to keep the way of the Lord by doing *righteousness* and *justice*." The opening line, "Shall I hide from Abraham what I am about to do?" signals to us that *God expects Abraham to respond* (Genesis 18:17-18, my translation from the Hebrew). Why would God share it with Abraham if God did not want Abraham to speak up? Then God uses two key words in describing Abraham's role in sustaining the covenant: righteousness and justice. A commitment to righteousness and justice is Abraham's responsibility in the covenantal partnership, and Abraham is still learning about what such responsibilities entail. Remember, this story occurs very soon after God first speaks to Abraham, very early in their relationship.

How does Abraham respond? Well, we can see that Abraham passed this subtle test with flying colors by looking at the words of his responses. Abraham answers by saying, "Will you sweep away the *righteous* with the wicked? . . . Far be it from You to do such a thing, to slay the *righteous* with the wicked so that the *righteous* fare as the wicked. Far be it from You. Shall not the *Judge* of the earth do *justice*?" (Genesis 18:25, my translation from the Hebrew). Abraham answers God with the exact words God used when he invited the challenge. He challenges God to pursue righteousness and justice, exactly as God had expected him to do. Abraham passed this test and grew through it, as he does so many other times.[9]

Thus, within the Hebrew Bible, what seems like a test of God serves as a test for us. This recognition is one of the reasons we continue to read and study the Bible. We are meant to put ourselves in the shoes of our biblical heroes. We are meant to ask ourselves how we would respond and fare in similar circumstances. This recognition helps us see another layer of depth to this last verse of the Lord's Prayer. *We may be tempted to consider ourselves above temptation.* This particular temptation frequently appears in Greek literature. It is a type of hubris, or excessive pride. We also see it in the Hebrew Bible. Most famously, Abraham's nephew Lot chooses to settle in the plains of Sodom and Gomorrah. In making that choice, Lot, according to the Jewish sages, felt he was above the wickedness of the town. He thought he could withstand its temptation and influence its people for the good. Yet, he slowly assimilated to his surroundings, and by the time Abraham visits him, he is among the town's leading citizens, as indicated when the Bible tells us he sat at the city gates. Such a place was reserved for leaders of ancient Near Eastern cities.

Lot demonstrates for us that we are all subject to what the Jewish sages called the *yetzer hatov*, the good inclination, and the *yetzer harah*, the evil inclination. A desire for righteousness and sin each exert a force within us. Both shape our character. The greatest rabbi of the Middle Ages, Moses Maimonides, taught that the laws and practices of Torah help the good inclination conquer the evil one. It does not destroy it but rather turns the energy of the evil inclination toward the doing of good. In other words, the good inclination wins by channeling the power of the evil inclination. It takes the energy of the evil inclination and uses it for the good.

A teaching from around the time of Jesus echoes this idea. The sages noted the repetition of the word *good* in the creation story. Each day is called good. Yet, the sixth day is called "very good." What explains the difference? *Why is that day special? They say the sixth day is special because the evil inclination was created that day.* Yet, if the evil inclination was created that day, why is the day called "very good"? Because without the evil inclination, the sages teach, people would not create families, build homes, and develop civilizations. The evil inclination is part of our life force.[10] We would be uncreative, unmotivated, and complacent without it. It is up to us to channel that evil inclination for the good. It is not purely a matter of grace. God cannot do it all for us. But neither is it purely a matter of will. Following the teachings of Torah unleashes the energy of the evil inclination toward the good. The Lord's Prayer is our plea to God to aid us in doing so.

CONCLUSION

The most reliable Greek manuscripts of the Gospel of Matthew do not contain the ending verse, "For thine is the kingdom, and the power, and the glory, for ever. Amen." This doxology probably emerged as the original Lord's Prayer was incorporated into the Christian liturgy. Its function resembles the verse "Blessed is God's glorious kingdom forever and ever" from the Shema. It is not part of the original text but has become associated liturgically with it.

Now that we know the deeply Jewish context of the Lord's Prayer, perhaps we can pray and understand it differently. We know the kingdom of heaven is not some far-off, abstract place. It is the world-to-come, which we can get a taste of every Sabbath. We know God's name is not some vague reference to the Divine. It is a symbol of God's power and reputation. We honor God's reputation—we magnify God's power—by how we live on earth. We know prayer is not simply a recitation of pretty words we say in church or synagogue. It is a way of speaking to God with our hearts and minds. It is a way of shaping ourselves so we can serve, in the phrase of the Jewish mystics, as vessels of holiness.

For me the most profound explanation of the way this works was given by the former Chief Rabbi of Great Britain Jonathan Sacks. He compared the influence of prayer on a person to the impact of water on a rock on the coastline. The water rolls over and over the rock. We cannot tell the difference it makes by looking at the rock after one day or even one week. Slowly but surely, however, the water smoothens out the rock. It reconfigures it. Ultimately, it transforms it.[11] Prayer can do the same for us. It does not instantly make us different people. In fact, we should be suspicious if it does. Over time, however, it remakes us. It smooths out the rough edges. It moves us closer to the core of our being—to the image of God within us. That is what prayer has and will always do.

CHAPTER 10

THE LAST DAYS

Jesus not only taught prayer but also, at the last moments of his life, uttered one drawn from the words of Psalm 22:1: "My God, my God, why have you forsaken me?" (my translation from the Hebrew). This prayer—in the form of a searing question—opens a window into the death and resurrection of Jesus, helping us see the Jewish influences and context in which his followers understood them. Followers of Jesus at the time drew from rich Jewish thinking on resurrection and life after death. Ultimately, Judaism and Christianity do part ways over the meaning of Jesus's death and resurrection. Yet, those who wrote and reflected on death and resurrection in the Gospels and other early writings were Jews. As we have learned, they saw and experienced Jesus as a Jewish teacher. They also understood the last moments of his life as expressing and fulfilling Jewish hopes and teachings.

Is this Jewish understanding of death and resurrection useful to Christians today? Absolutely. It is useful, I have discovered, in the same way experiencing and learning about the origins of Passover is useful to Jews. On Passover, we are meant to experience and feel what the ancient Israelites experienced and felt. We are meant to put ourselves in their shoes—to imagine that God freed *us* from Egypt. We felt the power of God's outstretched hand. We heard God's voice challenging the Pharaoh. We crossed the Red Sea from slavery to freedom.[1]

When reading and studying the Gospel accounts of Jesus's death, we can also try to put ourselves in the shoes of Jesus's followers. What were they feeling? What did they experience? What drove their reactions, their cries, their prayers? I first saw the connection between the Passover story and the last moments of Jesus's life two years ago, when I was preaching at a church. During the worship service, the congregation sang a song called "Were You There When They Crucified My Lord?" It was a moving hymn, and after the service I asked the pastor about it. She told me she sometimes tells the worshipers that the hymn asks us to imagine we ourselves are at the crucifixion. We ourselves are at the tomb. We are experiencing what the Gospels describe.

To better put ourselves in the shoes of early Jesus followers, we need to know what they believed, the texts they read, the framework through which they understood Jesus's life and death. It was a Jewish framework. More specifically, we can make sense of Jesus's final words on the cross by looking at them as a Jewish affirmation of faith. The resurrection reflected the yearning of first-century Jews. They yearned for a Messiah whose return would herald the end of death altogether, and the beginning of God's reign on earth. Knowing these beliefs helps us put ourselves in the shoes of those who were "there when they crucified my Lord."

JESUS'S LAST WORDS

As we noted earlier, Jesus asked many more questions than he answered. His most famous is the prayer expressed as a question on the cross, and they are among the last words he uttered: "My God, my God, why have you forsaken me?" Toward the very end of his life, Jesus asks this stirring question. They seem to question God's justice and care, saying God has forsaken him, abandoned him. Jesus seems to be losing faith at this critical hour. The theological problem is clear. How can one have comfort and faith in God's goodness if God forsakes Jesus at his time of need? How can Jesus be a model of faith if he believes God has forsaken him?

Some have argued that the word for "forsaken" has been mistranslated. It could mean something like "spare" or "kept" rather than "forsaken." Yet, this argument has many detractors. Furthermore, a precise biblical parallel exists with Jesus's last words. It is a direct quotation of King David in Psalm 22.

We can make sense of Jesus's question, however, when we view it through a Jewish theological lens. It is not a statement. It is a cry. It is not a declaration of faith. *It is a question emerging out of intimate love.* It fits squarely within the Jewish biblical tradition. The first hint of this truth is in the source of the quotation. King David had an intimate relationship with God. He, too, cried out several times. When King Saul pursued him; when his friend Jonathan was killed; when he

Just as God forgives the Pharaoh who murdered his people, Jesus forgives the Romans who murdered him. Forgiveness is possible even in the harshest of times.

and his men were on the run; at all of these times, David cried out to God.

Psalm 22 begins with those words, "My God, My God, why have You forsaken Me?" (NKJV). It continues with an expression of woe and fear. Yet, as he cries, David says God is not far away. God hears him. God will save him. *The cry turns into an affirmation. Because God is close—because God hears David's pain—God will respond.* Rather than signify lack of faith, the cry of despair testifies to God's presence and David's trust.

Think about it this way: a child cries because he or she knows a parent will respond. A cry of despair is not a proclamation of disbelief. Sometimes it can be the opposite. Sometimes God wants our tears as we experience the pain of the world. Sometimes a cry of despair, of questioning, is the best evidence of God's presence.

The reason many have trouble seeing this truth is that Christian theology has been shaped by the Greek philosophical tradition. Fundamental to Greek thought is Aristotle's idea of the excluded middle. Either a statement is true or its negation is true. Either God exists or doesn't exist. Either God has saved me, or God has forsaken me. This is very logical and coherent within its own intellectual framework. But faith does not operate in this intellectual framework. *Faith can feel a tension without resolving it.* In fact the refusal to resolve the tension is itself a sign of faith. The giants of faith in Judaism all issued cries of frustration.

Moses cries out in anger and pain when God refuses to let him into the Promised Land. He had spent his life leading the Israelites to freedom, but he could not experience it himself. Jeremiah cries out at God for seeming to reward the guilty and punish the innocent. Abraham even accuses God of potentially committing an injustice when he challenges God's decision to destroy Sodom and Gomorrah: "Shall not the Judge of the earth do justly?" (Genesis 18:25, my translation from the Hebrew). The more powerfully we feel the presence of God, the more passionately we will protest when injustice and wickedness seem triumphant. Jesus fits within this tradition. When he cries out, "My God, my God, why have you forsaken me?" he is expressing the cry of the Jewish giants of faith. He is asking a question that itself testifies to God's abiding presence.

THREE DAYS

Three days separate Jesus's death and resurrection. The Gospels portray Jesus prophesying this timing in the Gospel of Mark, where he says he will "be killed, and after three days rise again" (8:31, my translation from the Hebrew). In the following chapter, he envisions that he will be betrayed and killed, then "after three days, rise again" (Mark 9:31, my translation). Why three days? Does this timing echo an idea or theme from the Hebrew Bible? It does. Jesus refers to one of the biblical precedents for three days when he says in Matthew 12:41, "The citizens of Nineveh will stand up at the judgment with this generation and condemn it as guilty, because they changed their hearts and lives in response to Jonah's preaching. And look, someone greater than Jonah is here."

Jesus is referring here to the three days the Prophet Jonah spent in the belly of a whale. He was on his way to deliver a prophecy to the people of Nineveh. God had told Jonah the people of Nineveh needed to repent, and Jonah was God's messenger. Jews traditionally read the Book of Jonah on the

Yom Kippur, the Day of Atonement, the holiest day of the year. Jonah is a sign of God's readiness to forgive and renew our lives. He dwelled in the darkness of a whale for three days, yet he emerged ready to follow God and save the people of Nineveh.

The three days between Jesus's death and resurrection echo a similar theme. His followers experience a period of total darkness—like sitting in the belly of a whale—before a new emergence and life. A midrash—a Jewish legend—about Jonah and Nineveh also echoes the themes of forgiveness that Jesus preached in his final days. The midrash centers on the identity of the king of Nineveh. The text tells us he repents immediately, but it does not reveal his identity. The Jewish sages have a discussion of who he might be. They conclude he is Pharaoh from the Exodus story! This suggestion violates all the laws of space and time, of course. The exodus happened hundreds of years before the composition of the Book of Jonah. Yet, the spiritual lesson is profound. For Jews, Pharaoh is the symbol of human wickedness. He oppressed the people and had the Israelite firstborns thrown into the Nile River. Yet, according to the midrash, even the Pharaoh can repent and be forgiven.[2]

The parallel Jesus's followers likely made with the death of Jesus is striking. Just as God forgives the Pharaoh who murdered his people, Jesus forgives the Romans who murdered him. Forgiveness is possible even in the harshest of times.

RESURRECTION

The three days connect what is known in Holy Week as Good Friday and Easter Sunday. I recently asked my friend—

a more traditional Catholic priest—about why the Friday of Holy Week is called Good Friday. The feeling is not a good one. It commemorates Jesus's death. The good day, it seems, would be Easter Sunday. He told me that the goodness lies in the faith in the ultimate outcome. That Jesus's death is not really a death. It is, ultimately, a triumph over death. The resurrection celebrated on Easter Sunday affirms that message.

Most Jews today would say Judaism does not believe in resurrection of the dead. Yet, this belief reflects only the newer Jewish movements shaped in the nineteenth and early twentieth centuries. Reform Judaism, the largest Jewish denomination in America and the one in which I serve as a rabbi, embraced rationalism as a key criterion in how we understand Jewish beliefs and practices. Unfortunately, the kind of Judaism we teach in our synagogues and schools often skips over parts of faith like resurrection or the power of prayer that we cannot "prove" with science.

Many Reform Jews today believe Jews have never believed in ideas like resurrection or intercessory prayer. Yet, I always tell our students and congregants that the texts that shape Judaism convey a firm belief in the resurrection of the dead. One theology shaping the beliefs of Jews of first-century Judea and Galilee is what Professor E. P. Sanders calls "restoration eschatology." *Eschatology* refers to events that will happen at the end of history, and *restoration* refers to the return of Jewish sovereignty in Israel and a descendant of King David on its throne. Thus, restoration eschatology refers to the belief that we are near the end of days, and God will soon restore the Jewish people to sovereignty in its land with a Davidic king.[3]

This message resonated with first-century Jews because of the persecution experienced under Rome and its parallel with an earlier period of Jewish history. In the sixth century BCE, the Israelites had suffered under Babylonian domination. The Babylonians ultimately destroyed the First Jerusalem Temple. In the wake of its destruction, however, Jewish prophets preached both the continuation of one's life as a Jew outside of Israel and an eventual restoration of the Temple and a return to the land. Both of those visions came to pass, as the Persians ultimately defeated the Babylonians, and their king, Cyrus, allowed Jews to return to the land and rebuild the Temple. Faith that the Romans would be defeated and Jewish sovereignty restored helps us see why first-century Jews awaited a Messiah who would lead the way toward this restoration.

Resurrection is part of that restoration. Most of the Hebrew Bible has little to say about resurrection and the afterlife. We know that the "shades" of the dead, both good and wicked, reside in a place called *sheol*. Yet, we find little detail about what this place entails. We have no examples in the Hebrew Bible of God bringing individuals back to life. In the Prophetic books we do have some examples of healing, but Ezekiel is the clearest and most physically descriptive example of bodily resurrection.

In chapter 37 of the Book of Ezekiel, the Prophet envisions a valley full of dry bones. God tells him to speak to the bones and to tell them that God would breathe life into them, give them skin and flesh, and raise them into a great army. God then tells Ezekiel that the bones symbolize the people of Israel, who will rise again and return to their land. This vision has been extraordinarily influential in Jewish history. A key verse of the modern state of Israel's national anthem, "HaTikvah" (the Hope), is taken from it. The third verse of the anthem reads in Hebrew, "*Ode lo avdah tikvatenu; Hatikvah bat shnot alpayim.*" It means "our hope is not lost, the hope of two thousand years." In Ezekiel 37:11, the bones, symbolic of the Israelite people, speak to Ezekiel and say, "Our hope is lost; we are cut off" (my translation from the Hebrew). The national anthem echoes this verse by countering it, affirming that the hope was never lost. For the Jewish people, Ezekiel's prophecy came true.

It also rang true for followers of Jesus after his death. Several linguistic and historical clues point to its significance in the lives of his followers. First, the text is traditionally read during the week of Passover. Passover was the time when the Jewish people expected the Messiah to arrive. It was also the period when Jesus died and was resurrected. Thus, his death and resurrection parallels with the death and rebirth of the people of Israel in Ezekiel. Second, Ezekiel uses language familiar to the authors of the Gospels. Depending on your Bible translation, God constantly addresses Ezekiel as "Son of Man," a phrase Jesus often uses to describe himself. The phrase is used infrequently in the Hebrew Bible, found primarily in the books of Daniel and Ezekiel. It is also found in extra-biblical books from time, such as *Similitudes of Enoch*. It usually refers to the Messiah, a divine figure who appears to be human. The question here is not whether Ezekiel is a divine figure. For the Jewish people, he is not. He is simply a prophet. The language, however, points to messianic meaning. Ezekiel is predicting the rebirth of the Jewish people, an event that would accompany the arrival of the Messiah. Jesus's later reference to the "Son of Man" would thus connect his teaching to this passage.[4]

Perhaps the most significant message of this passage is its affirmation of bodily resurrection. God brings the bones to life and opens up their graves. The text is not purely a symbolic vision of rebirth. Its physicality points to the spirit giving life to the bodies of the dead.

Ezekiel's vision also points to the unity of the spiritual and political, which was part of the yearning of Jesus's followers. After the description of the dead leaving their graves, God asks Ezekiel to take two sticks and join them together as one, symbolizing the reuniting of the Northern Kingdom of Israel and the Southern Kingdom of Judah. They will be a "single nation in the land on Israel's highlands. There will be just one king for all of them. They will no longer be two nations, and they will no longer be divided into two kingdoms" (37:22). Their ruler will be a descendant of David, one who defeats both the worldly political powers and spiritual power of sin. As Ezekiel says, "They will no longer defile themselves with their idols or their worthless things or with any of their rebellions. I will deliver them from all the places where they sinned, and I will cleanse them. They will be my people, and I will be their God" (37:23). Thus, the resurrection of the Jewish people will lead to political independence and spiritual cleansing.

For first-century followers of Jesus, his resurrection served a similar purpose. It foretold the fall of Rome and a spiritual rebirth of the nations of the world. Indeed, whereas the resurrection in the Hebrew Bible foresaw the redemption only of the Jewish people, the resurrection of Jesus suggested a universal redemption.

Resurrection is a vindication of God's power and enduring truth of the covenant between God and Israel. It would not only bring back Jewish sovereignty in the land of Israel but also restore justice to the world. In other words, resurrection is an ally of justice. Those who had been oppressed would find themselves free and prosperous once again.

We cannot know for certain how widespread belief in restoration eschatology was, yet evidence suggests it was widely embraced. The historian Josephus, for example, points out that the biblical and extra-biblical books that promoted the idea—books like Daniel and Enoch—were particularly popular at the time. Jesus's resurrection would have been initially seen as the beginning of the broader restoration of the Jewish people. Jesus might have been seen as the Talmudic figure Nachshon.

Nachshon was one of the Israelite slaves in Egypt. According to Jewish legend, he was the first to step into the waters of the Red Sea before God parted them. He walked in the water all the way up to his eyes—nearly drowning—before God parted the sea, and Nachshon and the rest of the Israelites walked toward their freedom and redemption. From the perspective of the apostles and those witnessing the crucifixion and resurrection, Jesus was first in the walk toward redemption and freedom from Rome.

KING DAVID AND FREEDOM

The freedom and redemption envisioned by first-century Jews was not only political but also spiritual and social. The Jewish community of the first century was torn by internal conflict. As Josephus points out, the Pharisees, Sadducees, Essenes, and Zealots fought continually with one another.[5] Many yearned for a unifying figure who would restore spiritual solidarity and unity among the people. The models for such a figure included Moses and Ezra the scribe, who helped unify the people in the wake of the rebuilding of the Temple in the sixth century BCE. The figure echoed most frequently at Jesus's death, however, is King David.

As we noted earlier, at his death, Jesus quotes from Psalm 22, which tradition ascribes to King David. David is also linked in Jewish tradition with the Messiah and resurrection. Even today we frequently sing a Jewish song proclaiming "David, the King of Israel, is alive and ruling over us." David may have died physically, but he is alive among the Jewish people. He was remembered in the first century as the king who unified the twelve tribes of Israel. Jesus, with his twelve disciples, could unify, the thinking went, the fractured people of Israel.

> *Death is a reality we all face, but we can find spiritual nourishment in the idea that God conquers death. To believe death is not the end is to lessen our fear and pass from one form of life to another.*

David is also linked inextricably with the city of Jerusalem, where the crucifixion took place. Like Jesus, David is born in Bethlehem, yet he dies in Jerusalem. At his death, his work is not yet complete. This is true of all the great biblical leaders. Moses leads the Israelites out of Egypt and toward the Promised Land but never gets to enter into it. David pleads with God to allow him to build a great Temple in Jerusalem. The requirements and layout for the Temple had already been prescribed in the Book of Leviticus. This accomplishment would have culminated David's leadership of Israel.

God, however, refuses. David's work can only be completed by his son Solomon. For Christians, God's work can only be completed through his son, Jesus. And the salvation guaranteed by Jesus's death can only be achieved through resurrection. The two go together. And the Holy Spirit—the equivalent of the Temple Solomon builds—symbolizes God's abiding presence on earth after Jesus's death.

THE PARTING OF THE WAYS

Following the death of Jesus, however, his followers expanded the meaning of the Messiah to include salvation for all people. The Messiah became a figure of universal rather than particular redemption. This belief led ultimately to later followers of Jesus reaching out to gentiles to embrace their faith, inviting them into their community. This decision had far-reaching consequences. Judaism began as a people, a nation. We are the children of Abraham and Sarah. The Jewish people are known as *Bnei Yisrael*, which means the "Children of Israel." Israel is one of the names of Abraham's grandsons, Jacob, who is the father of the twelve tribes. When God calls Abraham, faith is a part of the culture of this new people, but there is not even a word for religion in the Hebrew Bible. Faith is linked indelibly with ethnicity. To become part of the Jewish people, one was either born into it or embraced its full way of life.

When Jewish followers of Jesus started to reach out to gentiles, they began to separate from the more traditional Jewish community. Scholars disagree over when this outreach began. What seems clear from the Book of Acts is that by the 50s CE, Jewish followers of Jesus and gentiles were eating at the same tables during ceremonial meals (see Acts 10). This detail reveals a growing comfort with gentile outreach, since adherence to the Jewish dietary laws would have prevented more traditional Jews from eating with non-Jews. Other examples followed, such as Peter's dream rejecting the necessity of maintaining the dietary laws and Paul's acceptance of converts who do not circumcise themselves. This development led to the eventual creation of a separate religion.

One other difference emerged as well. Traditional Jews did not subscribe to the notion of individual resurrection of the dead apart from wholesale resurrection of the entire nation of Israel. As Christianity developed and a larger resurrection did not happen, the number of Jewish followers diminished, and the number of gentiles who became Christian grew and began to outnumber the original Jewish followers. What remains from its Jewish origins, however, is the spiritual significance of resurrection. As Professor Jon Levenson points out in analyzing the beliefs of first-century Jews,

> Without the restoration of the people Israel, a flesh-and-blood people, God's promises to them remained unfulfilled, and the world remained unredeemed. . . . It is too often forgotten that the classical Jewish doctrine of resurrection does not represent a belief that death can be avoided, averted, or minimized. All to the contrary, it takes the gravity and tragedy of death with full seriousness and represents a belief that death will be—miraculously, supernaturally, graciously—*overcome*. Resurrection finds its place within a larger vision not of the continuation of the world but of its redemption.[6]

Regardless of our understanding of resurrection as individual or communal, we can find spiritual nourishment in the idea that God conquers death. Death is a reality we all face. As my grandfather used to joke well into his eighties, "There are only two things in life that are certain: death and taxes." To believe death is not the end is to lessen our fear. It is a way of passing from one form of life to another. To believe in some form of resurrection is also to believe our bodies are more than a collection of chemicals limited by nature. We are part of the natural world, but we are also part of eternity. Such a faith lets us see our lives differently. A belief in resurrection is not a form of self-delusion or magical thinking, as some writers and critics of religion have called it. Rather, it is a way of lifting us above our physical selves to see that we are something much larger and more enduring.

The vision of resurrection that Levenson describes became central to Christian understanding of Jesus and redemption. It did not become part of the Jewish national narrative. As a result, over many centuries, the Jewish context of Jesus's life and ministry was set aside or simply ignored. As we will learn in the following chapter, however, we are witnessing a renaissance in study and appreciation of the Jewishness of Jesus among both Jews and Christians. This renaissance continues to transform us and bring us greater understanding of our unique and shared beliefs and practices.

CHAPTER 11

FIVE RABBIS EXPLAIN JESUS

Jesus lived as a Jew. He prayed as a Jew. He died as a Jew. What, then, do Jews believe about him? The starting point for answering this question is a recognition, a recognition that Jesus's life and death became the foundation for a new religion. The relationship between that religion and the one into which Jesus was born has been filled with conflict. The reasons for this tragedy are complex, yet Jews and Christians have made enormous strides over the last one hundred years. I've seen it in my community, where we learn and study the Bible together. I've seen it in Israel, where we visit one another's sacred sites. And I've seen it in visits to the Holocaust museum in Washington, D.C., where the tragic consequences of hatred are starkly displayed. We have come closer to a world of mutual respect and understanding.

In seeking that understanding, I have been asked dozens if not hundreds of times what Jews believe about Jesus. Rarely is this question asked with any kind of agenda. Rather, it is asked with curiosity. The question comes not only from followers of

Jesus but also from Jews as well. The truth is that the question does not have a clear answer. It is a complex question and for every complex question, as H. L. Mencken purportedly put it, there is usually an answer that is "clear, simple, and wrong." So it is with what Jews believe about Jesus.

Despite this complexity, we need to try to answer it. We Jews have worked hard to improve Christian understanding of Judaism. So we need to learn more about the core beliefs of Christianity. And for the many Christians I know and have taught—especially those seeking to know more of and become closer to Jesus—learning what Jews believe about Jesus adds new layers of connection to his life. Since he was a rabbi, and an innovative one at that, rabbis are a terrific source for learning about what Jews believe. While scholars and historians can give us a critical and detailed picture of the first-century Jewish life in which Jesus lived and taught, rabbis can give us a better picture of his spirituality. They can help us understand what made him a rebel rabbi. What made his message resonate for Jews of the time? What spark of creativity ultimately led to the birth of a new religion? Fortunately, over the last one hundred years many rabbis have explored this issue, and the number of relevant books keeps growing. Here are five I find most persuasive and compelling.

A JEWISH NATIONAL HERO

Orthodox Rabbi Shmuley Boteach emphasizes Jesus's self-understanding and significance as a political leader of first-century Jews. As he has written, "The more we peel away the surface, the more we see the truth: Jesus was a great political leader who fought for the liberation of his people. In this sense, he saw himself in the guise of Moses and David, both of whom, while supremely concerned with the spiritual welfare of the people, were first and last concerned with the political freedom of the Jewish nation."[1] In other words, for Jews of the time, Jesus was a political hero and not a spiritual one.

This view has received further attention over the last few years in the wake of the publication of the best-selling book *Zealot*, by Muslim scholar of Christianity Reza Aslan.

> *God's truth rests with God. We simply do our best within the tradition we embrace to follow God's will here on earth.*

Aslan's argument is more nuanced than Boteach, suggesting Jesus was a radical in both political and religious views. Jesus, he argues, was a leading member of the first-century Jewish group known as the Zealots. Their political purpose was twofold: overthrow the Roman occupation of Palestine and restore the Law of Moses among its people.[2]

This view leads to distinct interpretations of Jesus's teachings. First, according to Aslan, proclamation of the kingdom of God has little to do with spiritual transformation. It has everything to do with political change. The kingdom of God was a replacement of Roman rule with Torah law. It was also the rooting out of the corrupt priests, whom the Zealots viewed as colluding with Rome. Although they shared the distaste for and distrust of the priesthood, the Zealots differed from the Pharisees in their refusal to compromise. The Zealots viewed other Jews who dared try to negotiate with Rome and seek some kind of coexistence as traitors. They took their cues from the Maccabees of the second century BCE, who viewed

Jews who adopted Hellenistic practices of dress and culture as enemies of Judaism.

Unfortunately, some of Aslan's and Boteach's focus on Jesus the zealot and national hero obscures the universalism of his teachings. Aslan is quite certain Jesus was exclusively concerned with Jews. As he has written, "If one wants to uncover what Jesus himself truly believed, one must never lose sight of this fundamental fact: *Jesus was not a Christian*. Jesus was a Jew preaching Judaism to other Jews. His was a Jewish mission, one concerned exclusively with the fate of his fellow Jews. Israel was all that mattered to Jesus."[3] While Aslan's focus on Jesus's Jewishness is commendable, it becomes triumphalist and dismissive of other points of view. Both Aslan and Boteach draw a sharp contrast between Jesus and the disciples who follow him, arguing that the disciples distorted his true Jewish teachings and turned a political zealot into a "celestial demigod." They reserve special scorn for the apostle Paul, who they say deemphasized Jesus's commitment to traditional Judaism and introduced a whole new focus on Jesus's divinity.

My problem is not with the history or research of the zealot school. It is with the way its supporters use the history to promote a theology. We can view Jesus as a Jewish national hero without descending into a biting critique of Paul and dismissal of the religion that emerged from his writings. For Jews, seeing Jesus as a nationalist hero of the first century puts him alongside other political leaders of the time such as Jochanan Ben Zakai, the founder of rabbinic Judaism. We can separate theology from history, appreciating the deep historical significance of Jesus and his influence on first-century Jews without embracing the beliefs of Christianity.

Jesus as a Jewish national hero may strike some Christians as unlikely and inconsistent with other parts of the Gospels. Jesus seems to oppose rebellion against Rome, as most famously noted in the teaching "Render unto Caesar what is Caesar's and unto God what is God's." Yet, it can also restore a mark of Jesus's Jewishness and help many see the extraordinary political and social circumstances in which Jesus lived. He lived during a time of political and spiritual upheaval. His teachings spoke to people surrounded by competing ideologies. Why is this knowledge important to our spiritual lives? Well, we better understand and appreciate a theologian like Dietrich Bonhoeffer when we recognize he protested the Nazis, was imprisoned, and was ultimately murdered during the Second World War. Similarly, knowing Jesus lived and taught amid conflict and controversy helps us better understand and appreciate his life, death, and teachings.

THE FIRST MESSIAH

Jesus as a Jewish national hero leads to no theological claims. Jesus is simply a great figure in Jewish history. Other rabbis, however, have gone a step further and engaged the claim of Jesus as Messiah. The word *messiah* is a complicated one. We often think of it simply as "savior" or God's chosen person to bring the world peace and harmony. The Hebrew word itself, however, means "anointed one," and it referred originally to the kings of Israel. An anointing with oil marked their ascension to the throne. Soon the phrase referred not just to Israel's earthly king but also to the heavenly king who would one day ascend to the throne and restore Jewish sovereignty in the land of Israel. That Messiah would be a descendant of Israel's greatest king, David. The Jews who followed Jesus in the first and second centuries had this conception of the Messiah, and this helps us understand the genealogy that opens the Gospel of Matthew explaining Jesus's descent from David.

As Christianity developed into a separate religion, Jewish thinking on the Messiah changed as well. The sages began to see the arrival of the Messiah as unfolding in two phases. The first phase would be marked by political and cultural turmoil, setting the stage for the arrival of the ultimate Messiah. The second phase would witness the Messiah's arrival and be marked by the rebuilding of the Temple in Jerusalem and the ingathering of the Jewish exiles from around the world in Israel. This messianic vision persisted in Jewish writings yet was emphasized little as Jews lived primarily as minorities with little political hopes and ambitions. Some rabbis saw the establishment of the state of Israel in 1948 as signaling the imminent arrival of the Messiah, yet that group remains marginal to the mainstream in Jewish life today.

In the last several decades, however, as the relationship between Jews and Christians has deepened and peaceful coexistence has become more imperative, the idea of the two-stage arrival of the Messiah has found new expression. Rabbi Yitz Greenberg, an Orthodox Jewish thinker whose theology is profoundly influenced by the Holocaust, suggested a new understanding of Jesus in Judaism. Greenberg calls Jesus the "failed Messiah," but "failed" is not meant to be pejorative. Moses failed to bring the Israelites into the Promised Land, yet he is revered. Jeremiah failed to get the Israelites to repent and ensure the survival of the Kingdom of Judah, yet he is revered. The "failed Messiah" description is meant to acknowledge the Jewish yearning for a Messiah in the first century. That Messiah would usher in world peace, the world envisioned by the Hebrew prophets. From a Jewish perspective, Jesus began that task but died before it was complete.[4]

Greenberg's theology reflects contemporary circumstances. For most of history, Jews could not affirm Christianity's messianic claims because it was seen to undermine Judaism and threaten our survival. Today, however, with a modern state of Israel and strong Jewish community, we can affirm the soundness for Christians of the messianism of Jesus. As Greenberg says,

> I think Jews have to be open to the idea that God speaks in different ways to different people. It's God's way of speaking to the gentiles, bringing them in parallel without replacing Judaism. Therefore Jews don't have to sit around trying to refute other religions. We can say firmly and respectfully, that the logic behind incarnation and God becoming flesh is the shared value system: Both religions believe that life will win out over death—resurrection is the climax of that process—because it's God's will that the world will be made perfect.[5]

Thus, while not accepting Jesus as the ultimate Messiah, Jews can see him as the Messiah of the first phase. Greenberg argues that some Christians implicitly accept this view by speaking of a second coming. A second coming acknowledges the first arrival did not complete the task. Greenberg's logic is extended by the late Rabbi Byron Sherwin, who draws from rabbinic tradition to identify Jesus as the "Messiah Ben Joseph," the Joseph Messiah. This is the Messiah of the first stage of messianic redemption. Jesus is a Jewish Messiah but not the final Jewish Messiah. Sherwin recognizes the controversial character of his argument, writing, "My radical suggestion is that [Jesus] may be considered a Jewish messiah, a failed rather than a false messiah, part of rather than apart from the life of his people and their messianic hope."[6] What is radical about this argument is that Sherwin places Jesus within the Jewish tradition. Jesus becomes part of the Jewish story.

Whether or not we embrace Greenberg and Sherwin, we can draw from the creativity and inclusive thrust of their suggestions. For Jews for too long, Jesus has been seen as divisive. I've had parents of a Jewish partner in an interfaith marriage beg me to tell the pastor at their child's wedding not to mention Jesus. When one of America's leading rabbis of the 1950s and 1960s, Maurice Eisendrath, suggested Jews could claim Jesus as a Jewish prophet, he was greeted with scorn.

The reason for this concern and scorn is largely fear of conversion and assimilation. Some Jews hear the word *Jesus* and immediately think of either anti-Semitism or someone trying to convert them to Christianity. While we need to remain wary of a world where anti-Semitism is on the rise, we do not need to see the name Jesus as a prod for conflict and withdrawal. Rather, the Jewishness of Jesus is a point of entry for meaningful dialogue and learning. For too long, dialogue has centered only on innocuous issues where we all agree. When we delve into one another's more fundamental beliefs, we can better appreciate and learn from one another. This learning can make us both more humble and honest. We are humble in that we see the depth and beauty of other faiths. We are more honest because we recognize our perspective is limited by our humanity. God's truth rests with God. We simply do our best within the tradition we embrace to follow God's will here on earth.

A Righteous Leader

Rabbis Zalman Schachter-Shalomi, a Jewish mystic, places Jesus in the category of a *tzadik*. A *tzadik* is a person of unusual righteousness who serves as a bridge between his community and God. He is meant to exemplify Jewish virtue. He is not God incarnate. Rather, he is "Torah incarnate." He is the Word made flesh, rather than God made flesh. According to Schachter-Shalomi, Jesus was an extraordinary leader within first-century Judaism. He was a counterpoint to the legalism of that era's influential rabbis, a model of piety rather than parochialism, of devotion rather than divinity.[7]

Thus, for Schachter-Shalomi Jesus is neither the first nor second Messiah. In fact, he believes the focus on Jesus as Messiah undercuts Jesus's profound message for Christians and Jews. The focus on Messiah turns Jesus's life into an absolute black-or-white question: either he is the Messiah or he is not. This hurts Christians, he says, by making Jesus too historical. Since conflict continues and the world remains divided, Jesus as the Jewish Messiah is difficult to sustain. It hurts Jews, he says, by putting him outside the boundaries of Judaism. Jesus, he argues, could add to the spirituality and richness of Jewish life, but not when the focus is solely on whether he is the Messiah or not.

If we set aside the idea of messiah, we can draw much from Jesus's life and teaching. We can see him as a living fusion of humanity and God's word, a living Torah. This is the definition of a tzadik. A tzadik teaches Torah not through lectures and classes but through imitating God in life. Schachter-Shalomi says the idea of a tzadik as "God's possibility for humanity in a physical body" is a plausible idea for "Jews of a mystical, aggadic, kabbalistic-hasidic persuasion."[8] In other words, for those pious Jews whose theology is shaped by mysticism and universalism, the notion of a living embodiment of God can make sense. The barrier to accepting this view of Jesus has been the insistence on believing he was the Messiah, and the long history of anti-Semitism and forced conversion. If we see him as a uniquely righteous person with much to teach, he can become more significant to Jews.

Emil Hirsch was one of several liberal rabbis who sought to place Jesus in the pantheon of Jewish prophets and teachers.

Part of the beauty of this approach is that it emphasizes action over theology. It is not what we believe about Jesus that is most important. It is about the way Jesus's life and death affect our own. It reflects a piece of wisdom I heard from a rabbinic mentor. "The sermon you give with your life," he said, "is more important than words you say from the pulpit." It is to the *life* of Jesus that we look for spiritual insights and not to the dogmas that arose after his death. This approach guided me in structuring this book. Rather than focus it around beliefs about Jesus, I structured it around his life. His life—as a Jew, reflecting and offering Jewish teachings—provides a way Jews and Christians can feel a deeper connection to Jesus.

Jews, as Schachter-Shalomi also points out, can see Jesus's teachings functioning in the first century in a way similar to how Hasidic Judaism reshaped eighteenth- and nineteenth-century Judaism. The Judaism of that period was heavily focused on textual learning. The measure of a scholar and of true piety was mastery of the Talmud and its laws and interpretations. The Hasidic movement arose in opposition to this focus, deliberately choosing to emphasize prayer, dance, and enhanced worship rather than study. One famous Hasidic teaching praises the man who prays with his prayer book open backward. Even though he cannot read or understand the words, his heart is attuned to God.

In the first century, Jesus may have played a similar role within the Jewish community. The priesthood had become corrupt. Others had left and gone to the caves of Qumran, where they produced the Dead Sea Scrolls. And the Pharisees, while champions of the people and likely the group to which Jesus was closest, had their own internal struggles. Jesus may have been a voice seeking to restore the piety of traditional Judaism.

A LIBERAL RABBI

While Jesus lived a traditional Jewish life, his followers introduced significant changes to it. Most famously, the apostle Paul permitted the consumption of nonkosher food and entry of uncircumcised gentiles into the Jewish community. These changes helped facilitate the split between the more traditional Jewish community and the emerging group of Jesus's followers. From a modern perspective, however, we can see Paul as introducing changes into traditional Judaism that many Jews today embrace. More specifically, Reform Judaism does not require Jews to follow the kosher laws or perform the traditional circumcision ritual on the eighth day. Now, certainly we encourage both practices, but they are not at the core of Jewish life as they were in the first century. We have also de-emphasized ritual and the significance of the law and replaced it with focus on ethics and community. In other words, aside from the divinity of Jesus, Paul's teaching would have been perfectly acceptable to many modern Jews.

Many Reform rabbis of the late nineteenth and early twentieth centuries made this argument in an effort to reclaim Jesus as a liberal Jew. Among the most prominent was a Chicago rabbi named Emil Hirsch. Considered the most learned and eloquent liberal rabbi, he wrote, "[Jesus] was of us; he is of us. We quote the rabbis of the Talmud; shall we then, not also quote the rabbi of Bethlehem? Shall not he in whom there burned, if it burned in any one, the spirit and the light of Judaism, be reclaimed by the synagogue?"[9] Hirsch was one of several liberal rabbis who sought to place Jesus in the pantheon of Jewish prophets and teachers. They argued that the Sermon on the Mount, for example, should be studied at Jewish religious schools as an expression of the Jewish prophetic tradition.

The problem with these proposals at the time was that anti-Semitism still played an outsized role in American Christianity. The idea that Jews killed Jesus and that Christians had replaced Jews as God's chosen people made its way into Christian sermons, textbooks, and among prominent public preachers such as Father Charles Coughlin of Detroit. Many Jews saw Jesus through this context, viewing those who believe in him as inclined toward belittling Jews and Judaism. Suspicion of attempts to convert Jews to Christianity also made it difficult to accept such proposals to embrace Jesus as a Jew. Many other Jewish leaders argued Jews needed to learn more about traditional Jewish holidays and practices rather than the Jewishness of Jesus. Proposals like those of Hirsch generally went unheeded.

Today, however, where anti-Semitism is on the decline in America and Jews are more self-confident in their Jewishness, a fresh look at Jesus as a liberal Jew is possible and useful. We can look at some of the ideas taught and promoted by Jesus in ways that can enrich Jewish identity and expression. One possibility, for example, is the emphasis on social justice. Early rabbinic Judaism talks little about justice within the larger society. Jews were barely tolerated minorities and were concerned more with survival than with social teachings.

Jesus's teachings on social justice, however, fill the New Testament and reflect a biblical perspective meaningful to contemporary Jews. Jesus's embrace of the immigrant, the outsider, and others marginal in first-century Jewish life can also inspire Jews today. Jews can make the case—as Kaufmann Kohler, one of the early champions of Reform Judaism, did—that Jesus was a "helper of the poor" and a "sympathizing friend of the fallen."[10] Jesus learned these values at the synagogue and brought them to the forefront of first-century Jewish life.

A Bridge

More than 50 percent of American Jews marry someone who is not Jewish. As both my wife (who is a rabbi) and I have seen, many struggle to figure out the role of faith in their families. When both partners take their faith seriously, they need to find ways to teach and practice their religion without confusing their children. This is not easy. In fact, many give up. I have seen many parents who care about their faiths simply do nothing with their children because it is too difficult. Such families could use rituals and ideas that can help bridge their faiths without sacrificing the beauty and depth of either one.

The name Jesus can today serve as a bridge instead of serving as a source of division, as it has for so many Jews for hundreds of years. Jews can see him as a Jewish leader and teacher who never abandoned his Judaism. Christians can see him as the central teacher and focus of devotion. Sometimes this is harder for the Jewish partner because Christianity includes the Old Testament as part of its Bible. Thus, Christians can see Jesus within Judaism more naturally. Jesus is not part of the Jewish Bible or its literature. Yet, a focus on deeds, holidays, and learning rather than doctrine can help bridge this divide. The life of Jesus—emphasizing the deeds and teachings at its core—can be part of that bridge.

EPILOGUE

A few years ago, following a lecture I gave at a local church, a student confessed to me that she wished she had been born a Jew so she could know what Jesus experienced. Moved by her words, I asked her what—aside from being reborn in a different era—could help her gain that knowledge. She said, "A real understanding of Jesus's life as a Jew." This book is the result of that conversation. It is a result of thousands of hours spent in learning and conversations with devoted Jews and Christians who care about growing in faith and knowledge.

I hope seeing Jesus's life as a Jew opens up new ways of appreciating and growing closer to him. I hope it helps Christians move beyond the simple understanding of Jesus as a ticket to heaven to Jesus as a way of living within a tradition and relating to others. I hope it helps Jews move beyond a simple association of Jesus with anti-Semitism to Jesus as a teacher of Judaism. I also hope it creates new encounters with God and with one another.

As people of faith, our challenge is to try not to undermine one another. It is not to try to prove our faith superior to every other. It is living and teaching our message of life and hope in a world filled with violence and indifference. It is finding and articulating faith in ourselves. In such a world, the more we learn from one another, the more confident and knowledgeable we can be in living our faith.

Victor Hugo once said, "All the forces in the world are not as powerful as an idea whose time has come." Seeing Jesus as a Jew is an idea whose time has come.

NOTES

1. A Humble Birth

1. *Babylonian Talmud, Tractate Shavuot*, 35b.
2. Jonathan Sacks, "Even Higher Than Angels," www.rabbisacks .org/covenant-conversation-vayera-even-higher-than-angels/.

2. An Unexpected Turn

1. Martin Buber, *The Legend of the Baal-Shem*, 1995 ed. (New York: Schocken, 1955), 36.
2. *Babylonian Talmud, Tractate Brachot*, 20a.
3. Mark Sheridan, *Genesis 12–50*, vol. 2 of *Ancient Christian Commentary on Scripture: Old Testament*, ed. Thomas C. Oden (Downer's Grove, IL: IVP Academic, 2002).
4. Rabbi David Wolpe, foreword to *Jesus the Jewish Theologian*, by Brad Young (Grand Rapids: Baker Academic, 1991), xiv.

3. Entering the Waters

1. See Josephus, "Essenes," in *The Jewish Wars*, bk. 2, chap. 8. Available at http://ancienthistory.about.com/od/josephus/l/bl_jose phus_JW_essenes.htm.
2. *Mekhilta Bahodesh* 4, II 227.
3. Attributed to the late Rabbi Louis Finkelstein.
4. James Carroll, *Christ Actually: The Son of God for the Secular Age* (New York: Viking, 2014), 117.
5. Varda Polak-Sahm, *The House of Secrets: The Hidden World of the Mikveh* (Boston: Beacon, 2009), xxi.

4. Surviving a Wilderness of Temptations

1. Genesis Rabbah, 8:5.

2. *Babylonian Talmud, Tractate Bava Batra*, 16a.

3. Amy-Jill Levine and Marc Z. Brettler, *The Jewish Annotated New Testament* (Oxford: Oxford University Press, 2011), 2.

5. Calling the Disciples

1. *Babylonian Talmud, Tractate Bava Matzia*, 84a.

2. Malcolm Gladwell, *Blink: The Power of Thinking Without Thinking* (New York: Back Bay, 2007).

3. *Babylonian Talmud, Tractate Brachot*, 1a.

4. Martin Copenhaver, *Jesus Is the Question: The 307 Questions Jesus Asked and the 3 He Answered* (Nashville: Abingdon Press, 2014).

5. See Bruce Feiler, *The Secrets of Happy Families* (New York: William Morrow, 2013).

6. David Flusser, *The Sage from Galilee: Rediscovering Jesus' Genius*, 4th ed. (Grand Rapids: Eerdmans, 2007), 77.

7. Flusser, *Sage from Galilee*, 80.

6. Do You Believe in Miracles?

1. The story is recounted in the *Babylonian Talmud, Tractate Brachot*, 19a.

2. The story is recounted in David Flusser, *The Sage from Galilee: Rediscovering Jesus' Genius*, 4th ed. (Grand Rapids: Eerdmans, 2007), 97–98.

3. Jonathan Sacks, *The Great Partnership* (New York: Schocken, 2014), 168.

7. Finding Honey on the Page

1. *Ethics of the Fathers*, chap. 1, v. 14.

2. Martin Buber, *I and Thou* (New York: Scribner, 1958), 25.

8. The Shema

1. This is according to Rabbi Jason Miller. See http://blog.rabbi jason.com/2010/10/justin-bieber-says-Shema-other-jewish.html.

2. Norman Lamm, *The Shema: Spirituality and Law in Judaism* (Philadelphia: Jewish Publication Society, 2000), 13.

3. Anton Chekhov, "Misery," in *The Short Stories of Anton Chekhov,* ed. Robert N. Linscott (New York: Modern Library, 1959).

4. Benedict de Spinoza, *The Ethics*, part V, prop. XXIII.

5. See *The Torah of Rav Kook*, http://ravkooktorah.org/VAET_64.htm.

6. See Michele Cushatt, *Undone* (Grand Rapids: Zondervan, 2015).

7. Martin Luther King Jr., "Speech at the Great March on Detroit," 1963, available at http://mlk-kpp01.stanford.edu/index.php/encyclopedia/documentsentry/doc_speech_at_the_great_march_on_detroit/.

8. *Babylonian Talmud, Tractate Berachot*, 61b.

9. Steve Jobs, "You've Got to Find What You Love," *Stanford Report* (June 14, 2005), available at http://news.stanford.edu/news/2005/june15/jobs-061505.html.

10. Shraga Simmons, "Shema Yisrael," available at www.aish.com/jl/m/pb/48954656.html.

9. The Lord's Prayer

1. Amy-Jill Levine, *The Misunderstood Jew* (New York: HarperOne, 2007), 12.

2. Ibid., 42.

3. *Mekhilta of Rabbi Simeon bar Yohai* to Exodus 13:21, p. 47.

4. Mark 12:17; *Babylonian Talmud, Tractate Baba Batra*, 54b. My translations.

5. Josephus, *Antiquities*, 13:172.

6. Levine, *Misunderstood Jew*, 47.

7. *Babylonian Talmud, Tractate Avot*, 4:21.

8. Levine, *Misunderstood Jew*, 50–51.

9. For further exploration of this text, see Jonathan Sacks, *To Heal a Fractured World* (New York: Continuum, 2007), 18–20.

10. *Babylonian Talmud, Tractate Brakhot*, 32a.

11. Jonathan Sacks, *The Koren Siddur* (Jerusalem: Koren, 2009), xliv.

10. The Last Days

1. I explore this idea more fully in *What Every Christian Needs to Know About Passover* (Nashville: Abingdon Press, 2015).

2. "Pharaoh in Nineveh," *JewishAnswers.org*, www.jewishan swers.org/ask-the-rabbi-category/jewish-texts/?p=2683. The blog post quotes *Pirkei D'Rabbi Eliezer*, Exod. 14:31.

3. See a discussion of these ideas in Michael F. Bird, *Jesus and the Origins of the Gentile Mission* (New York: Continuum, 1988), 30.

4. Some translations do not use "Son of Man" but rather "The Human One."

5. Josephus, *Antiquities*, 13.

6. Jon D. Levenson, *Resurrection and the Restoration of Israel: The Ultimate Victory of the God of Life* (New Haven, CT: Yale University Press, 2006), x.

11. Five Rabbis Explain Jesus

1. Shmuley Boteach, *Kosher Jesus* (Jerusalem: Gefen, 2012), 51.

2. See Reza Aslan, *Zealot: The Life and Times of Jesus of Nazareth* (New York: Random House, 2014).

3. Ibid., 121.

4. See Shaul Magid, "The New Jewish Reclamation of Jesus in Late Twentieth-Century America," in Zev Garber, ed., *The Jewish Jesus: Revelation, Reflection, Reclamation* (Purdue: Purdue University Press, 2011), 358–82.

5. Alice Chasan, "Disagreeing in the Service of God," 2006, available at www.beliefnet.com/Faiths/2006/03/Disagreeing-In-The -Service-Of-God.aspx#0Ds3BGZuXyZz1pEg.99.

6. Magid, "New Jewish Reclamation," 367.

7. Ibid., 370.

8. Ibid., 371.

9. George L. Berlin, *Defending the Faith: Nineteenth-Century American Jewish Writings on Christianity and Jesus* (Albany: State University of New York Press, 1989), 141.

10. Magid, "New Jewish Reclamation," 365.

Please enjoy the first chapter from Rabbi Evan Moffic's previous book *What Every Christian Needs to Know About Passover*, available at retailers including AbingdonPress.com and Cokesbury.com.

CHAPTER 1

FROM SLAVERY TO FREEDOM

The Biblical Exodus

Sometimes our most important journeys begin in tragic circumstances. It may be the death of a loved one. It may be the loss of a job. We can feel trapped by these circumstances, and they can start to define us. I recall a member of a synagogue I served in Louisiana who had lost her husband tragically. She was in her sixties and quite healthy. She had many friends and a successful career. When her husband died, however, her life became defined by this loss. She took all the paintings down from the walls of her house, and replaced them with pictures of him. She changed her stationery to identify herself by her husband's first and last name. She even kept his voice on her answering machine.

Now contrast my Louisiana friend's journey with that of another parishioner from Chicago. She also experienced the loss of her husband at a relatively early age. He was a force of nature, a highly successful businessman and community leader. She mourned deeply. Many of their friends had been through him, and thus she felt somewhat disconnected from the wider community after his death. Yet, after about a year, she began to change. She started volunteering at a hospital and a grief counseling center. She became involved in the synagogue, which had earlier been a peripheral part of her life. She began a new path defined by the future rather than the past.

All of us grieve differently, and I probably should not judge someone for her feelings of loss. But it seems clear that the second parishioner found a healthier and more satisfying path. She experienced monumental pain, but she did not let tragedy define her future.

What meaning do we make out of tragedy and loss? That is the question that my two parishioners' experiences of bereavement pose to me. And it is also one of the fundamental questions of Passover. The Israelites had experienced profound individual and social loss through decades of enslavement, and God miraculously freed them—and then commanded them to observe a holiday in which they were to make some sort of sense, some sort of meaning, from their loss. God didn't tell the Israelites to forget their suffering in Egypt, or to just "move on." Rather, God told them to remember forever that they were slaves in Egypt. The Passover celebration is the medium through which Jews, over the centuries, have remembered and made meaning from the trauma of slavery.

Like my two parishioners, the ancient Israelites' journey began in tragic circumstances. After having lived as welcome residents of Egypt for hundreds of years, they are enslaved by a pharaoh determined to destroy them. They experience four hundred years of bitter slavery. Yet, after God leads them to freedom, they do not define themselves as victims. They do not seek revenge on the Egyptians. Rather, they hold the first sacred Passover meal telling their story of God's redemption. They derive the moral requirement to never oppress the stranger because they had been strangers in the land of Egypt. In other words, they seek to experience the blessing of freedom and not the pain of victimhood.

They begin their new journey by gathering for the Passover meal, the oldest religious ritual in Western history, in which they tell a story that redefines who they are.

How did the Israelites transform themselves? What role did God play in their journey? How did they use memory and ritual to reframe the experience of slavery? Let's look at their story.

How Did the Jewish People End Up in Egypt?

The Jewish people arrived in Egypt 430 years before the Exodus. They came with the support of the then pharaoh, whose kingdom had been saved through the foresight and prophecy of the Israelite Joseph. Joseph was the second youngest of the Jewish patriarch Jacob's twelve sons. After being sold into slavery by his brothers, who were jealous of his special talents and their father's overt favoring of him, Joseph had used his wits and abilities to arrive at a position of power in Egypt. He served as Pharaoh's prime minister, saving Egypt from a seven-year famine that destroyed much of the surrounding area.

For a while, Joseph's descendants prosper in Egypt. Then, according to the Book of Exodus, "a new king came to power in Egypt who didn't know Joseph" (Exodus 1:8). This formulation is the Bible's way of telling us that this pharaoh did not know of the great contributions that the Israelite Joseph made to Egypt. He did not know the history of the Jewish people in the land. He was like a type of person we all know: someone who looks at others and asks only "what have you done for me lately?" Soon the pharaoh becomes paranoid. Fearing the growth of a non-native, non-Egyptian population that could turn against Egypt in times of war and also looking for cheap labor, this pharaoh enslaves the Israelites, demanding they work in building Egyptian cities and monuments. Pharaoh sought to destroy Israelite culture and unity so that they would not pose a threat to native Egyptians.

Despite these efforts to annihilate them, the Israelites survive. According to later biblical commentary, their population actually grows, and they become more unified as a people. They continue to use Hebrew names and refuse to succumb to Pharaoh's destructive policy. Their enslavement continues for four hundred years, but they remain a distinct people. They do not let persecution and hatred change who they are.

Four hundred years after slavery begins, however, a new pharaoh determines to destroy the Israelites once and for all. He decides to throw every male child born to an Israelite into the Nile River, thus draining their strength and eliminating future generations. Despite their efforts at maintaining their inner and outer strength, the Israelites feel despondent. They reach a bottom, seeing their future wiped out before them.

In any journey, however, the bottom has one advantage. There is nowhere to go but up. And it is at their bottom that the Israelites cry out to God, and God hears their cry. God answers their cry through the figure of Moses. Moses renews the Israelites' hope. He renews their faith. And he shows them that though they may have been enslaved, faith can set them free.

WHO IS MOSES?

In Jewish tradition Moses is the greatest prophet the Jewish people ever had. He is the lawgiver, teacher, and scribe of God. He challenges Pharaoh, leads the people through the desert, and guides them to the edge of the Promised Land. His life ends on a poignant note, as God permits him to see the Promised Land from afar but not to enter it. Moses' final resting place is unknown because, according to the Jewish sages, God did not want the people to turn Moses into a divine figure. He is simply the Jewish people's greatest prophet. His story is the story of the Exodus.

Moses' birth seems to suggest he was destined for great things. Unlike the other Israelites, he never experiences slavery. He is born during the time when Pharaoh is killing all Israelite males at birth. Immediately after his birth, however, Moses' mother and sister place him on a basket and send it floating down the Nile River. His sister Miriam watches the basket from reeds beside the river, and she sees the daughter of Pharaoh take the basket and find the Hebrew child. In the Bible, Pharaoh's daughter has no name, but later Jewish commentators call her *Batya*, which means "daughter of God."

Her compassion and humanity lead her to adopt Moses as her own son. She also hires Moses' mother and sister as his nurse and nanny, unaware of who they really are. Moses is raised in Pharaoh's palace, a "prince of Egypt," presumably afforded all the luxuries and opportunities of Egyptian royalty.

Everything changes the day he first leaves the royal palace. His age at the time is unknown, but later interpreters suggest he was fifteen. He sees Egyptian taskmasters whipping Israelite slaves. Although the text does not tell us how and when he learned he was an Israelite, Moses somehow knows the slaves are his people, and he acts to defend them. He kills one of the Egyptian taskmasters. The next day he sees a fight between two of the Israelite slaves. One of them taunts him and says, "Are you planning to kill me like you killed the Egyptian?" (Exodus 2:14) Moses realizes that word of his crime has begun to spread, and he will be a wanted man in Egypt. He flees for Midian, which is a desert land of shepherds and nomads. His first stop is at a well. He encounters a group of hostile shepherds attacking a group of seven sisters. Moses defends them and drives the shepherds away. He returns with the daughters to their home and meets their father, Jethro, a local priest. Moses soon marries one of the sisters he saved named Zipporah.

Each of these stories is significant because it reveals the core of Moses' character. He could not bear seeing a helpless slave beaten by an Egyptian taskmaster. He could not stay silent as two Israelites fought one another. And he could not stand by as Midianite shepherds attacked a group of defenseless sisters. *Moses does not stand idly by as others suffer and bleed. He is present. He is present to suffering. He is present to injustice. And he is present to God.*

HOW GOD MET MOSES

We see this presence to God most clearly in the next forma-tive incident in Moses' life. The Bible tells us that while Moses was out walking with his flock, he hears God's voice speaking from a bush that burns but is not consumed (Exodus 3:1-12). Moses had to be present to hear that voice. In fact, the Jewish sages write that this bush had been burning without being consumed for years. Most people, however, did not notice it. They simply walked by. Moses noticed the burning bush and wondered why it was not consumed. When he turned around and paid attention to it, God spoke to him. His attunement to divine power made him worthy of leadership. Others had their opportunities. But Moses responded. The Hebrew word he used in answering God's voice highlights his readiness to act. Moses says "*Hineni*, I'm here" (Exodus 3:4).

What does God tell Moses? According to the text, God has now "clearly seen" Israel's oppression at the hands of the Egyptians (Exodus 3:7). God has chosen Moses to lead the Israelites to freedom. God reminds Moses that he is an Israelite and that his ancestors Abraham, Isaac, and Jacob were God's faithful servants. God tells Moses his time to act and lead has arrived.

WHO IS GOD?

When Moses turned, he had a profound, dramatic, and in some ways quite intimate encounter with God—and the Bible's description of the encounter between God and Moses also reveals a core part of how Jews understand God. In an enigmatic verse, God says to Moses that he can tell the people that "*Ehyeh asher Ehyeh*" sent him (Exodus 3:14). This particular divine name—*Ehyeh asher Ehyeh* (אֶהְיֶה אֲשֶׁר אֶהְיֶה)—does not occur anywhere else in the Bible. It does not even seem like a proper name. In Hebrew the phase means "I will be what I will be." Some English Bibles translate it as "I am Who I am." Or "I am What I am." The Hebrew is written, however, in the future tense: "I will be what I will be," or "I will become what I will become."

Why does this difference matter? How might it shape our own understanding of God? I believe it teaches us how the Bible wishes us to understand God. God is not static. God is dynamic. God is not defined by the past. God is experienced in the future. *What I will be, God is telling Moses, depends on what you and the people do. God is a becoming, and not just a being.* In fact, the Hebrew language does not have any word like the English "is." In Judaism, as reflected in the Hebrew language, identity is never static, and never unalterable. Like God, we are dynamic, evolving, ever changing, and ever growing. We may have had a miserable upbringing. We may have done things in the past we are not proud of. But those things do not define us. We define ourselves in the future. And the future shapes how we are remembered.

My favorite example of this truth is physicist Alfred Nobel. He invented dynamite and made a tremendous fortune. When he died, however, he left that fortune to create a prize for a person or group that best promotes peace. And we remember his name through that prize—the Nobel Peace Prize. God is telling Moses—just as he is telling us—your journey is not over. Your people will not be slaves forever. With God's help, they will become free. God cares about who we will become, not just who we have been. God sees our potential and invites us into the future.

God's revelation to Moses also gives Moses confidence. He hears God's instruction, and finds a strength he did not know he had. After God appears to him at the burning bush, Moses is no different physically. Yet, he is different spiritually. After having hesitated and feeling unsure about the work God has for him, Moses accepts God's call, and he returns to the Egyptian royal palace. He comes before Pharaoh and tells him "This is what the LORD, Israel's God, says: 'Let my people go'" (Exodus 5:1). Pharaoh's first response seems to convey genuine shock. This shepherd, whom he had probably known as a boy growing up in the royal palace, is demanding he free a huge population of slaves. He does so in the name of the Israelite God, while Pharaoh sees himself as a god. To put it in contemporary nonreligious terms, it would be as if a farmer from a poor and distant country like Bangladesh demands that the president of the United States do something at the behest of the president of Bangladesh. Pharaoh understandably challenges Moses' request. "Who is this LORD whom I'm supposed to obey by letting Israel go? I don't know this LORD, and I certainly won't let Israel go," he replies (Exodus 5:2).

Moses and Aaron repeat their demand. Pharaoh refuses, and chides them for distracting the Israelites from their labor. He demands they leave and then tells the chief Egyptian taskmaster to toughen the Israelite labor requirements. In particular, he tells the taskmaster to take away the straw the Israelites used for making bricks, but still require they make the same number of bricks each day. They would have to go out and find their own straw, making their labor longer and more strenuous.

Pharaoh seems to be trying to turn the Israelites against Moses by punishing them for Moses' impetuous behavior.

The ploy works. They blame the messenger. They beg Pharaoh to relent, and he tells them they are lazy. They swear at Moses, telling him God will judge him harshly for his actions. These criticisms are the first of many Moses receives as he leads the Israelites out of Egypt. He pleads to God for guidance, and God tells him to keep doing what he is doing. God is telling Moses to be patient because God has larger plans. God is setting up the confrontation with Pharaoh that will lead to freedom. God then tells Moses to return to Pharaoh and demand once again that Pharaoh free the Israelites.

An emboldened Pharaoh responds by daring Moses and Aaron to prove the power of their God and perform a miracle. Aaron takes his staff and turns it into a snake. Pharaoh's magicians do the same thing, but their snake is eaten by Aaron's. Still, Pharaoh remains unmoved. He rejects Moses' demands to free the Israelites. God then inflicts the first of ten plagues upon the Egyptians. He turns the Nile River into blood. The Nile is the life source of Egypt. It waters its crops and serves as Egypt's source of influence. Turning it to blood undermines Egypt's strength. Yet, Pharaoh dismisses it as an amateur trick his magicians could do. His heart remains unmoved.

God's next plague is to cover the land of Egypt with frogs. Pharaoh begs Moses to stop it, promising to free the Israelites when the frogs are gone. Moses does so, but then Pharaoh reneges on his promise. In describing these events, the Bible emphasizes that God knew Pharaoh would renege. Indeed, God hardened Pharaoh's heart, ensuring he would resist letting the Israelites go free and the plagues would continue.

I have always been troubled by this idea that God hardened Pharaoh's heart. Does that mean God takes away Pharaoh's free will? Does that mean God desired the plagues to continue so as to inflict massive destruction on Egypt? It seems that way. What kind of God would do that?

These questions have stumped Jewish interpreters for centuries. The most accepted answer is that God hardening Pharaoh's heart allowed Pharaoh to continue to follow his heart's true desires. He did not want to give in. But the harshness of the plagues and the growing opposition of his courtiers tempted him to simply accede to Moses' requests. *God therefore preserved Pharaoh's free will—his desire to continue to enslave the Israelites—by hardening his heart and making him incapable of turning back from confrontation with Moses.*

Other theologians suggest Pharaoh lost his free will during the first six plagues. Free will is not absolute. Pharaoh had six chances to repent. When he did not do so, his character had become so corrupted that he lost the ability to change course. It was as if he became caught in a spider web and could not get out of it. God did not need to harden Pharaoh's heart because it was already a solid rock. By saying God hardened Pharaoh's heart, the Bible is simply emphasizing how wicked Pharaoh was.[1]

I don't find any of these answers completely convincing. The best response I can give to the text is to suggest it teaches the difference between Moses and Pharaoh. Moses attunes himself to God's word. He is present to God at the burning bush and his life is transformed. Pharaoh, on the other hand,

---

1. This point of view is outlined in psychologist Erich Fromm's classic text *Escape from Freedom* (New York: Holt, 1994).

has a hardened heart. He cannot listen. He is not present. He is indifferent. Both Moses and Pharaoh hear the same God. But they respond differently. By highlighting these differences, the Bible is trying to teach us how to open ourselves to God's presence. We are to be like Moses—present, engaged, listening, letting God guide us in the unfolding of our journey, rather than closing our hearts as Pharaoh did.

> *Both Moses and Pharaoh hear the same God, but they respond differently. The Bible teaches us how we are to be like Moses—present, engaged, listening, letting God guide us in the unfolding of our journey, rather than closing our hearts as Pharaoh did.*

By opening ourselves up to God on our journey, we also open ourselves up to one another. This teaching helps us understand the ninth plague, the enclosing of Egypt in total darkness. The darkness was so thick that "people couldn't see each other" (10:23). This verse cannot mean only physical darkness. If that was case, people could just light lamps. Rather, *it was a darkness that infected the heart and soul.* Physically, the Egyptians were able to see, but psychologically and spiritually, they were not able to feel or care for one another. This is what the Torah means when it says the "people couldn't see each other." They were blind to one another's needs. Each person acted for and saw only himself or herself.

Perhaps the Bible is suggesting that a total absence of faith in our lives can make us blind to one another's needs. Pharaoh and the Egyptians were utterly indifferent to God's voice and commandments. Thus, they became utterly indifferent to one another.

THE MOST GRUESOME PLAGUE

The final plague haunts us to this day. It is the death of all the firstborn sons in Egypt. It happens on the night when Israelites put blood from a lamb on the doors of their homes so that the angel of death would "pass over" them on its journey through Egypt. This plague works. It leads Pharaoh to relent and let the Israelites leave. Still, it leaves us with many questions.

Why hurt thousands of Egyptian families on account of the intransigence of Pharaoh? God seems to be inflicting collective punishment on a gruesome scale. What did the firstborn sons of Egypt have to do with enslaving the Israelites? Is God condoning the death of innocent Egyptians? Does Passover celebrate those deaths?

The Jewish sages struggled with these questions. Through the ritual of Passover, however, they offered a compelling answer. During the Passover meal, when the plagues are recounted, we let a drop of wine fall from our wineglasses for each plague. For the final plague, we let two drops spill. The drops represent the tears of the Egyptians. They suffered because of their despotic leader, and we respond with empathy. When others suffer, we do not rejoice. We do not take pleasure in others' pain. We open our hearts and share their tears.

A TRANSFORMATIVE MOMENT

The tenth plague devastates Pharaoh, and he agrees to let the Israelites leave. Pharaoh, however, soon changes his mind, as God said he would, and leads an army in pursuit of the Israelites. The army catches up with them, and by the time the Israelites reach the shores of the Red Sea, they are terrified. The plagues and hasty march will end in their death and destruction.

Then their journey reaches a transformative moment. They witness a miracle. As Pharaoh's army closes in, God splits open the sea. The Israelites cross, and the sea closes in on Pharaoh's troops. As they reach the banks of the other side of the sea, the Israelites begin to sing a song of freedom. They dance. They celebrate.

This scene of redemption is engraved on our minds. Why is it there? Surely God could have simply whisked the Israelites across. Why the drama of opening and closing the waters of the sea? I believe it teaches us that sometimes, extraordinary inexplicable things happen on our journey. And when these things happen, we can only stand in awe and sing God's praise. We can all have these experiences, and they do not have to be as dramatic as the splitting open of the sea.

I remember sitting one day with my three-year-old daughter. She had a book in her hands and was turning the pages and telling the story. This was her regular habit. She could not yet read the words, but she could tell the story based on the pictures. I had one ear listening to her voice and the other, I am sorry to say, thinking about the coming week's sermon. Suddenly I stopped thinking about the sermon. I turned my head toward her. Something was different. I looked down at the book. I realized she was not telling the story in her own words. *She was reading the words on the page.* I couldn't believe it. Time stood still for a second. Then I looked at her, laughed, smiled, and started to sing. I didn't sing any particular song. It was just words of joy and happiness, and we both started dancing around the room. That was a transformative moment. *It was a time on my journey when the waters parted and I glimpsed God working in the world.* By splitting open the sea in front of the entire Israelite people, God is telling us we can all have those moments. We only have to be present and attune our souls to recognize them.

My daughter's learning to read was not the end of her journey. It was just the beginning. In fact, the next night I asked her to read a different book for me. She replied by telling me she did not know how to read. She wanted me to read to her. This continued for several nights. Knowing how to read was exciting but also a little scary. The same was true for the Israelites. The crossing of the sea was magnificent, but now they faced forty years of wandering in the wilderness. They began to have doubts. They started to backslide. They cursed Moses and pleaded for the comfort and security of Egypt. How did they make it through this part of their journey? What kept their faith? We will discover the answers they gave—and the truths they teach us—in the next chapter.

Want to learn more about Rabbi Evan Moffic
and check out other great books from
Abingdon Press?

Check out our website at
www.AbingdonPress.com
to read interviews with your favorite authors,
find tips for starting a reading group,
and stay posted on what new titles are on the horizon.

Be sure to visit Rabbi Moffic online!
www.rabbimoffic.com

This meal is the oldest religious ritual in Western history and holds the power to renew one's life and faith. Now popular speaker and author Rabbi Evan Moffic shares the Passover observance with twenty-first-century readers.

Reading this book will change the way you celebrate communion and Easter. It will give you a taste of an ancient ceremony Jesus faithfully celebrated. And it will help you discover what message this sacred story holds for you. You will understand the radical claim that one meal—one momentous meal—can, in fact, change your life.

ISBN 978-1-4267-9156-7

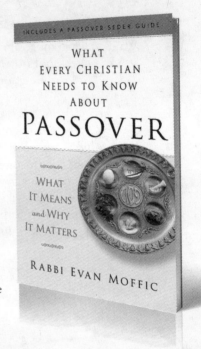

"Vividly written and full of history and insights. It is an experience rich in cultural definition that will heighten and enlighten your own faith walk."
—**Patsy Clairmont**, author of *Twirl: A Fresh Spin at Life*

"The spiritual roots of every Christian go back to Jesus, and the spiritual roots of Jesus go back to Judaism, and the spiritual roots of Judaism are sunk deep in the promise and practice of liberation. Rabbi Evan's What Every Christian Needs to Know About Passover is a wonderful way to water those roots."
—**Rabbi Rami Shapiro**, author of *Let Us Break Bread Together: A Passover Haggadah for Christians*

"Passover is a universal story of freedom whose message is needed now more than ever. Rabbi Moffic opens us to this Jewish holiday in a way that can speak to people of all faiths."
—**Lonnie Nasatir**, Anti-Defamation League

FURTHER PRAISE FOR RABBI EVAN MOFFIC

"People everywhere are seeking a better way to live. Many have a faith tradition we call home—but sometimes moving outside that tradition helps us see resources we never knew were there. Through his stories and insight, Rabbi Evan Moffic shines the light of Jewish wisdom in a way that helps all of us find our way."
—**Reverend Christine Chakoian**, Senior Pastor, First Presbyterian Church of Lake Forest

"Rabbi Moffic has given us a generous guide to unlocking the power of our words—to God, ourselves, and each other."
—**Jeff Goins**, author of *Wrecked: When a Broken World Slams into Your Comfortable Life*

"Rabbi Moffic is an engaging teacher who excels at communicating ancient truths for modern audiences. His insights into Hebrew scriptures and the Jewish heritage of the Christian faith will be a blessing to all who want to learn."
—**Pastor Steve Gillen**, Willow Creek Community Church

"Rabbi Moffic is a captivating speaker for people of all ages. He shows the richness of the Old Testament and Judaism and gives insights into Jesus' Jewish context and character. Christians and Jews can benefit from his knowledge and from his character."
—**Ken Davis**, humorist and best-selling author

"Evan Moffic unlocks the wisdom of Judaism in a way that can enrich us all."
—**Dr. Eboo Patel**, founder and President, Interfaith Youth Core

"Evan Moffic is a rabbi, but he's also an extraordinary scholar and a teacher of the highest order. He can speak to us all, whatever our faith or culture. And he does it with grace, humor, and erudition. Such a guy."
—**Jim Kenney**, International Interreligious Peace Council,
    Interreligious Engagement Project, Common Ground

"Rabbi Moffic is one of the best young Rabbis and scholars I have ever heard speak and teach about both Judaism and Christianity. His wit, his humor, and his deep knowledge about the Old Testament and early Christianity will give insight into Jesus' Jewish context, history, and character."
—**Newton Minow**, former chairman of the Federal Communications
    Commission (FCC), Vice-Chair Commission on Presidential Debates